An Analysis of

John P. Kotter's

Leading Change

Yaamina Salman
with
Nick Broten

Published by Macat International Ltd
24:13 Coda Centre, 189 Munster Road, London SW6 6AW.

Distributed exclusively by Routledge
2 Park Square, Milton Park, Abingdon, Oxon OX14 4RN
711 Third Avenue, New York, NY 10017, USA

Routledge is an imprint of the Taylor & Francis Group, an informa business

Copyright © 2017 by Macat International Ltd
Macat International has asserted its right under the Copyright, Designs and Patents Act
1988 to be identified as the copyright holder of this work.

The print publication is protected by copyright. Prior to any prohibited reproduction, storage in
a retrieval system, distribution or transmission in any form or by any means, electronic, mechanical, recording or otherwise, permission should be obtained from the publisher or where
applicable a license permitting restricted copying in the United Kingdom should be obtained
from the Copyright Licensing Agency Ltd, Barnard's Inn, 86 Fetter Lane, London EC4A 1EN, UK.

The ePublication is protected by copyright and must not be copied, reproduced, transferred,
distributed, leased, licensed or publicly performed or used in any way except as specifically
permitted in writing by the publishers, as allowed under the terms and conditions under which
it was purchased, or as strictly permitted by applicable copyright law. Any unauthorised distribution or use of this text may be a direct infringement of the authors and the publishers' rights
and those responsible may be liable in law accordingly.

www.macat.com
info@macat.com

Cataloguing in Publication Data
A catalogue record for this book is available from the British Library.
Library of Congress Cataloguing-in-Publication Data is available upon request.
Cover illustration: Etienne Gilfillan

ISBN 978-1-912302-14-7 (hardback)
ISBN 978-1-912127-22-1 (paperback)
ISBN 978-1-912281-02-2 (e-book)

Notice
The information in this book is designed to orientate readers of the work under analysis,
to elucidate and contextualise its key ideas and themes, and to aid in the development
of critical thinking skills. It is not meant to be used, nor should it be used, as a
substitute for original thinking or in place of original writing or research. References and
notes are provided for informational purposes and their presence does not constitute
endorsement of the information or opinions therein. This book is presented solely for
educational purposes. It is sold on the understanding that the publisher is not engaged
to provide any scholarly advice. The publisher has made every effort to ensure that
this book is accurate and up-to-date, but makes no warranties or representations with
regard to the completeness or reliability of the information it contains. The information
and the opinions provided herein are not guaranteed or warranted to produce particular
results and may not be suitable for students of every ability. The publisher shall not be
liable for any loss, damage or disruption arising from any errors or omissions, or from
the use of this book, including, but not limited to, special, incidental, consequential or
other damages caused, or alleged to have been caused, directly or indirectly, by the
information contained within.

CONTENTS

THE MACAT LIBRARY

The Macat Library is a series of unique academic explorations of seminal works in the humanities and social sciences – books and papers that have had a significant and widely recognised impact on their disciplines. It has been created to serve as much more than just a summary of what lies between the covers of a great book. It illuminates and explores the influences on, ideas of, and impact of that book. Our goal is to offer a learning resource that encourages critical thinking and fosters a better, deeper understanding of important ideas.

Each publication is divided into three Sections: Influences, Ideas, and Impact. Each Section has four Modules. These explore every important facet of the work, and the responses to it.

This Section-Module structure makes a Macat Library book easy to use, but it has another important feature. Because each Macat book is written to the same format, it is possible (and encouraged!) to cross-reference multiple Macat books along the same lines of inquiry or research. This allows the reader to open up interesting interdisciplinary pathways.

To further aid your reading, lists of glossary terms and people mentioned are included at the end of this book (these are indicated by an asterisk [*] throughout) – as well as a list of works cited.

Macat has worked with the University of Cambridge to identify the elements of critical thinking and understand the ways in which six different skills combine to enable effective thinking.
Three allow us to fully understand a problem; three more give us the tools to solve it. Together, these six skills make up the **PACIER** model of critical thinking. They are:

ANALYSIS – understanding how an argument is built
EVALUATION – exploring the strengths and weaknesses of an argument
INTERPRETATION – understanding issues of meaning

CREATIVE THINKING – coming up with new ideas and fresh connections
PROBLEM-SOLVING – producing strong solutions
REASONING – creating strong arguments

To find out more, visit **WWW.MACAT.COM.**

CRITICAL THINKING AND *LEADING CHANGE*

Primary critical thinking skill: ANALYSIS
Secondary critical thinking skill: EVALUATION

John P. Kotter's *Leading Change: Why Transformation Efforts Fail* is a classic of business literature, and a strong example of high-level analysis and evaluation.

In critical thinking, analysis is all about the sequence and features of arguments; when combined with evaluation of the strengths and weaknesses of an argument, it provides the perfect basis for understanding corporate strategies and direction. Kotter applied these skills to his own experience of coaching large and small businesses through changes aimed at improving their performance. At heart, his conclusion was simple: unsuccessful transformations usually result from poor management decisions.

Kotter's view was that it was not enough for executives to have management skills. Strong leadership is required, together with a clear process that can be used by all kinds of companies and organizations, no matter what sector they are operating in. Reassessing his own successes and failures alike, Kotter then deployed his analytical skills to understand the sequence and features of both sets of experiences before evaluating the strengths and weaknesses that had contributed to outcomes both good and bad. From there, he distilled lessons that help to identify the common mistakes that managers make when they try to implement change.

The process allowed Kotter to develop an eight-stage model for successful organizational transformation – a model still widely used twenty years on.

ABOUT THE AUTHOR OF THE ORIGINAL WORK

John P. Kotter is a highly respected academic and business consultant with many years of practical experience advising major US corporations on change. Born in 1947, he has degrees from Massachusetts Institute of Technology and Harvard University, and is currently professor of leadership at Harvard. His company, Kotter International, consults for large corporations such as Microsoft, and for US government agencies. Kotter's work is characterized by its down-to-earth tone, using practical examples to advise those in all walks of organizational life who must grapple with change.

ABOUT THE AUTHORS OF THE ANALYSIS

Dr Yaamina Salman holds a PhD in organisational management from the University of Edinburgh. She is currently teaching at the Institute of Administrative Sciences at the University of the Punjab in Pakistan.

Nick Broten was educated at the California Institute of Technology and the London School of Economics. He is doing postgraduate work at the Pardee RAND Graduate School, and works as an assistant policy analyst at RAND. His current policy interests include designing distribution methods for end-of-life care, closing labour market skill gaps, and understanding biases in risk-taking by venture capitalists.

ABOUT MACAT

GREAT WORKS FOR CRITICAL THINKING

Macat is focused on making the ideas of the world's great thinkers accessible and comprehensible to everybody, everywhere, in ways that promote the development of enhanced critical thinking skills.

It works with leading academics from the world's top universities to produce new analyses that focus on the ideas and the impact of the most influential works ever written across a wide variety of academic disciplines. Each of the works that sit at the heart of its growing library is an enduring example of great thinking. But by setting them in context – and looking at the influences that shaped their authors, as well as the responses they provoked – Macat encourages readers to look at these classics and game-changers with fresh eyes. Readers learn to think, engage and challenge their ideas, rather than simply accepting them.

'Macat offers an amazing first-of-its-kind tool for interdisciplinary learning and research. Its focus on works that transformed their disciplines and its rigorous approach, drawing on the world's leading experts and educational institutions, opens up a world-class education to anyone.'

Andreas Schleicher
Director for Education and Skills, Organisation for Economic Co-operation and Development

'Macat is taking on some of the major challenges in university education … They have drawn together a strong team of active academics who are producing teaching materials that are novel in the breadth of their approach.'

Prof Lord Broers,
former Vice-Chancellor of the University of Cambridge

'The Macat vision is exceptionally exciting. It focuses upon new modes of learning which analyse and explain seminal texts which have profoundly influenced world thinking and so social and economic development. It promotes the kind of critical thinking which is essential for any society and economy. This is the learning of the future.'

Rt Hon Charles Clarke, former UK Secretary of State for Education

'The Macat analyses provide immediate access to the critical conversation surrounding the books that have shaped their respective discipline, which will make them an invaluable resource to all of those, students and teachers, working in the field.'

Professor William Tronzo, University of California at San Diego

WAYS IN TO THE TEXT

KEY POINTS

- Born in 1947, John P. Kotter is an American management consultant* and scholar who currently teaches leadership* and management* at Harvard Business School and consults through his firm, Kotter International.

- *Leading Change* presents a comprehensive, eight-step model for how to carry out organizational change in large corporations.

- The book's use of practical examples and its wide applicability has made it one of the most influential books on organizational transformation ever written.

Who Is John P. Kotter?

John P. Kotter is an iconic figure in the field of organizational change and transformation, both as an academic and as a professional. He has written extensively on the topic and is widely read and acknowledged by managers and academics alike. He is often referred to as a "change and management guru."[1] In his writing, Kotter draws heavily on his practical experiences working with corporate organizations as a management consultant. The basis of his work throughout his career has been the translation of lessons he has learned about leadership and management from consulting and from study into recommendations that can be put into action. Managing transformation has been one of his major preoccupations for decades. In *Leading Change*, as in much of his work, Kotter opts for a conversational tone, using anecdote and analysis as if he were speaking directly to an audience of executives and business leaders.

Born in 1947, Kotter holds degrees from the Massachusetts Institute of Technology (MIT) and Harvard Business School, where he completed his PhD in 1972. He became a full professor at Harvard in 1980 at the age of 33, making him one of the youngest in the university's history. He continues to serve at Harvard as Konosuke Matsushita Professor of Leadership, Emeritus, teaching leadership and management. In addition to his academic work, Kotter is also chairman of Kotter International, a consulting firm he co-founded in 2008. The company has a broad client base, from large corporations such as Allstate, Genentech, and Microsoft, to governmental agencies such as the US Naval Air Systems Command and the Royal Canadian Navy.[2]

What Does *Leading Change* Say?

There are two core parts to *Leading Change,* which was first published in 1996. First, Kotter discusses what he sees as the eight most common mistakes companies make when trying to make changes. These are:

1. Tolerating complacency and failure to create a sense of urgency.
2. Failure to develop an effective coalition (an alliance of like-minded individuals).
3. Failure to construct a sensible vision.
4. Failure to communicate that vision.
5. Allowing obstacles, such as organizational structure and reluctant   employees, to block the vision.
6. Failure to build on short-term successes.
7. Declaring victory too soon.
8. Not embedding successful changes in the corporate culture.*

Kotter notes that "none of these change errors would be that costly in a slower-moving and less competitive world."[3] However, in a rapidly changing economy, "making any of the eight errors common to transformation efforts can have serious consequences."[4] Changes that move too slowly can cause layoffs, budgetary squeezes, and have lasting effects on communities where the company exists.

To guide companies away from these errors, Kotter details an eight-step process for leading change that must be carried out in sequence:

1. Establish a sense of urgency.
2. Create the guiding coalition.*
3. Develop a vision and strategy.
4. Communicate the change vision.
5. Empower broad-based action.*
6. Generate short-term wins.*
7. Consolidate gains and produce more change.
8. Anchor new approaches in the culture.[5]

Another important feature of Kotter's change process is the distinction between management and leadership. He says "successful transformation is 70 to 90 percent leadership and only 10 to 30 percent management."[6] In a slower world, he argues, managerial talent was perhaps more important than leadership: "For most of this century, as we created thousands and thousands of large organizations for the first time in human history, we didn't have enough good managers to keep all those bureaucracies functioning."[7] By contrast, in an age of technological and industrial transformation, the "sacrifice, dedication, and creativity"[8] necessary for change must come from leaders rather than managers.

The core of *Leading Change* is Kotter's elaboration on the eight-step process and the practical examples he discusses to make the steps relatable. A typical example is his discussion of "Jerry," an "overworked division-level CFO (Chief Financial Officer) at a major oil company"[9] in the chapter on building a guiding coalition. Jerry is more "manager than leader" and is "naturally suspicious of calls for significant change." So it may initially seem not worth the effort to convert him to support a change process. He is likely to resist, and will probably not offer creative solutions.[10] If Jerry has some rank or status in the company, however, because of his seniority and experience, ignoring him or excluding him from a change effort will eventually backfire, so Kotter advises leaders to include "Jerry" in their planning. *Leading Change* is full of characters like Jerry, and to a large extent the success of the book is due to the relevance of these characters and their situations.

Why Does *Leading Change* Matter?

Leading Change is a valuable text for many different people. Business students who know something of the problems associated with organizational transformation will be able to relate directly to the examples and concepts in the book. Such students may benefit from examining Kotter's examples as if they were genuine business cases: What is the market under analysis? Who are the characters involved? And how does Kotter explain the mistakes the characters make? Business students with ambitions towards leadership positions will learn the methods of one of the most influential change consultants of the last two decades. It is likely that students who fully absorb Kotter's approach will be able to interact more effectively with their own bosses when they enter the workplace.

The book is also of use to non-business students. Most of the principles in *Leading Change* apply equally well to any organizational setting. For example, Kotter advises change leaders trying to communicate their vision to "keep it simple" with "focused, jargon-free information" and to use "the power of metaphor, analogy, example, or just plain colorful language to communicate complicated ideas quickly and effectively."[11] He presents this advice in the context of a change effort in a large company, but it could equally well be applied to a start-up, a new marketing campaign, a congressional campaign, or a major research initiative in a university. Readers of all kinds who work in groups, regardless of their size or function, will find invaluable information in *Leading Change*.

Kotter instinctively values leadership over management. The "lifelong learner"* model Kotter presents at the end of the book is a challenge to continue to grow, both personally and professionally, throughout life. By using the concept of compounded growth* (growth that builds on itself) to describe personal development, Kotter suggests that significant transformations can result from small behavioral changes such as asking for critical feedback or taking risks.[12] *Leading Change* can serve as both business manual and self-help book.

NOTES

1 "Kotter's 8-Step Change Model," Mind Tools, accessed May 21, 2015, http://www.mindtools.com/pages/article/newPPM_82.htm.

2 "Our Clients," Kotter International, accessed May 17, 2015, http://www.kotterinternational.com/clients/.

3 John P. Kotter, *Leading Change* (Boston: Harvard Business School Press, 1996), 15.

4 Kotter, *Leading Change*, 15.

5 Kotter, *Leading Change*, 20–2.

6 Kotter, *Leading Change*, 26.

7 Kotter, *Leading Change*, 27.

8 Kotter, *Leading Change*, 30.

9 Kotter, *Leading Change*, 60.

10 Kotter, *Leading Change*, 60.

11 Kotter, *Leading Change*, 91–2.

SECTION 1
INFLUENCES

MODULE 1
THE AUTHOR AND THE
HISTORICAL CONTEXT

KEY POINTS

- *Leading Change* presents an eight-stage process to implement successful change in organizations.

- Kotter's experience as a management consultant* in many different industries makes his book both unique and practically useful.

- The book was first published in 1996 at a time of increasing globalization* and increasing uncertainty about how this would change ways of doing business.

Why Read This Text?

John P. Kotter wrote *Leading Change* in 1996, after his well-received article "Leading Change: Why Transformation Efforts Fail,"[1] published in the March–April 1995 issue of *Harvard Business Review*. The book, which has won many awards and is an international bestseller, is considered a landmark publication in the area of leadership* and change. Its central idea is to present an eight-stage process to implement change and aid transformation efforts in organizations, based on the author's personal experience of helping big businesses. The term "big" is important—Kotter's focus in *Leading Change* is transforming large firms, not small companies.

The book's practical tone and presentation is its key strength. Rather than focusing on academic arguments, Kotter presents his change principles clearly and succinctly, regularly using examples from real but mostly anonymous firms to support his ideas. The breadth of examples makes the book a useful guide for a wide audience. While

> **❝** By any objective measure, the amount of significant, often traumatic change in organizations has grown tremendously over the past two decades. Although some people predict that most of the reengineering, restrategizing, mergers, downsizing, quality efforts, and cultural renewal projects will soon disappear, I think that is highly unlikely … As a result, more and more organizations will be pushed to reduce costs, improve the quality of products and services, locate new opportunities for growth, and increase productivity. **❞**
>
> John Kotter, *Leading Change*

not all readers will identify with each of the eight stages Kotter describes, it is likely that readers with experience in big firms will find at least some of his suggestions useful. *Leading Change* is also notable for its foresight. Kotter sets his argument about organizational change in the context of an increasingly global and fast-changing business environment. Today, his concerns about how to deal with rapid changes are even more appropriate.

Author's Life

John P. Kotter was born in 1947. He graduated from the Massachusetts Institute of Technology (MIT) in Electrical Engineering and Computer Science in 1968, then went on to do a Master of Science from MIT and later a Doctorate in Business Administration from Harvard Business School. In 1972, Kotter joined the faculty of the Harvard Business School, where he was named full professor in 1980 at the age of 33. He continues to teach there today.

Over the course of his career, Kotter has written 18 books, including *Our Iceberg is Melting*, a *New York Times* bestseller published in 2006. In 2001, *Business Week* magazine named Kotter the premier leadership guru in the United States, based on a survey of 504 enterprises.[2] He is also the founder of Kotter International, which helps Global 5000 companies*—a database of 5000 corporations representing more than \$50 trillion in revenue—implement change using the eight-step process introduced in this book.

According to Kotter, *Leading Change* draws exclusively on his own experiences as a business consultant with almost 100 companies over a period of 25 years. As he writes in the preface to the book: "This work is more personal than any I've previously published. I'm communicating here what I've seen, heard, and concluded on a set of interrelated topics that appear to be increasingly important."[3] Little is known publicly about the exact nature of Kotter's consulting work or the relationships he has with the companies in his examples. But he is internationally renowned in the area of leadership and change management. His position as a thought leader on organizational change gives credibility to his interpretations of these real-world cases.

Author's Background

Kotter's work has been influenced by globalization, which is characterized by rapid technological change,* international economic integration,* the evolution of domestic markets* in more developed countries, and the collapse of communism.* The modern wave of globalization that began in the 1980s and forms the backdrop of *Leading Change* is tied to a number of events, including a series of free-trade* agreements that dismantled global trade barriers, reduced transport costs, and led to the willingness of companies to look abroad to lower production costs.

Kotter argues that because companies are not immune to global economic and social forces, they have had to embrace organizational change more intensely. Whereas businesses in the pre-globalized twentieth century may have been able to survive for several decades with very little internal transformation, Kotter suggests that is no longer the case now that markets are global. He writes: "Even companies that sell only in small geographic regions can feel the impact of globalization. The influence route is sometimes indirect: Toyota beats General Motors (GM), GM lays off employees, belt-tightening employees demand cheaper services from the corner dry cleaner."[4] This example highlights the potential unintended consequences of business decisions in a global marketplace. While Toyota was acting in its own interest only, its decisions had a direct impact on GM, which then had an indirect impact on many small businesses, including the dry cleaners that serviced GM employees.

NOTES

1   John P. Kotter, "Leading Change: Why Transformation Efforts Fail," *Harvard Business Review* 73, no. 2 (1995): 59–67.

2   "Rating the Management Gurus," Bloomberg, October 14, 2001, accessed May 18, 2015, http://www.bloomberg.com/bw/stories/2001-10-14/rating-the-management-gurus.

3   John P. Kotter, *Leading Change* (Boston: Harvard Business School Press, 1996), x.

4   Kotter, *Leading Change*, 18.

MODULE 2
ACADEMIC CONTEXT

KEY POINTS

- The study of management* concerns the planning, structure, design, and effectiveness of institutions, particularly business organizations; by focusing on change efforts, *Leading Change* relates to many of these topics.

- Prior to Kotter's work, management studies* had shifted from focusing on objectives to studying relationships between employers and employees.

- Kotter based *Leading Change* on his own work, but was likely influenced by others developing similar change models at the same time.

The Work in its Context

John P. Kotter's *Leading Change* is an example of management studies, an area of business thought focused on understanding how organizations, specifically firms, plan and organize their resources to achieve their goals. A related, and in some cases overlapping, discipline is leadership studies,* which focuses on the role of leadership* in carrying out organizational objectives. Management and leadership studies can be loosely grouped into two categories: one is characterized by highly theoretical, sometimes mathematical studies of organizational behavior;* the other consists of practical guides intended for business leaders. *Leading Change* is an example of the second category.

Leading Change also fits into the more general area of business and administration literature. Scholarly writing in this tradition can be both analytic and prescriptive, aimed at both academic and professional audiences. For example, an author may conduct an extensive research

> **❝** Management is doing things right. Leadership is doing the right things. **❞**
>
> Peter Drucker, *Essential Drucker: Management, the Individual, and Society*

project, including surveys and statistical analysis, to determine how incentives in a firm influence performance. This kind of analysis would include observed results similar to those found in economics* and political science.* Another author may write a guidebook for managers during times of uncertainty using real-world examples and the author's own intuition. By its very nature, business literature is highly diverse, runs across numerous disciplines, and tends to overlap with areas of economics, sociology, mathematics, and history.

Overview of the Field

The modern academic study of management is often traced back to the work of Peter Drucker,* an Austrian American management consultant* and academic. Drucker's most notable contribution to the field was the Management by Objectives (MBO)* approach, which he described in his 1954 book, *The Practice of Management.* The MBO approach tasks managers with making decisions that lead the organization to specific results, taking into account changing external circumstances such as fluctuations in the economy and the behavior of other firms in the market. Drucker suggests that only by defining objectives beforehand can decisions be made effectively. He writes: "Objectives are needed in every area where performance and results directly and vitally affect the survival and prosperity of the business."[1] While managers may prefer to make decisions as simply and as free from judgment as possible—restricting the range of choices available so as to minimize errors—Drucker holds that applying judgment is one of the most important aspects of successful management.

Another scholar who contributed to the early development of management and leadership studies was Douglas McGregor,* whose book, *The Human Side of Enterprise*, published in 1960, introduced the Theory X and Theory Y* model of individual motivation.[2] In this context, "theory" refers to the assumptions managers make about their employees—in other words, managers tend to treat their employees in a certain way according to a preconceived theory about what motivates them. According to McGregor, Theory X employees are lazy and unmotivated, and so need close supervision, while Theory Y employees are ambitious and self-motivated. McGregor's work introduced managers to the idea that company performance can be affected by their own assumptions about employees' motivations. It also brought concepts from psychology and human behavior into management literature.

Academic Influences
During the 1990s, when Kotter developed the ideas for *Leading Change*, there was already a growing body of literature about so-called learning organizations* (valuing teamwork and collaborative models of management), organizational change, and transformation in general. For example, W. Warner Burke* and George Litwin* developed a model to understand the features common to successful change efforts.[3] Unlike Kotter's book, Burke and Litwin's paper explores the factors that *cause* change, not how managers can better bring about change. Similarly, Heather Haveman* wrote a paper in 1992 that argued against the position that change was harmful to an organization's performance. She suggested instead that "organizational change may benefit organizational performance and survival chances if it occurs in response to dramatic restructuring of environmental conditions and if it builds on established routines and competencies."[4] In other words: when circumstances require change, it will tend to be good for the company; when they do not, change may be harmful.

Some authors at the time, such as Peter Senge* and William Edwards Deming,* were also talking about quality control, teamwork, and adaptive organizations in the context of change efforts.[5] Senge and Deming both recognized the importance of globalization* and the challenges it represented. Indeed, one of Deming's suggestions to managers in a complex, global economy was to "eliminate management by objectives" and "substitute leadership."[6] Kotter was undoubtedly influenced by these writers and, while not responding directly to them in *Leading Change*, he incorporated some of their ideas into the book. It should be noted, however, that Kotter's work was predominantly based on his own experiences and intuition, not on the work of others.

NOTES

1   Peter Drucker, *The Practice of Management* (New York: Harper Collins, 1954), 63.

2   Douglas McGregor, *The Human Side of Enterprise* (New York: McGraw-Hill, 1960).

3   W. Warner Burke and George H. Litwin, "A Causal Model of Organizational Performance and Change," *Journal of Management* 18, no. 3 (1992): 523–45.

4   Heather A. Haveman, "Between a Rock and a Hard Place: Organizational Change and Performance Under Conditions of Fundamental Environmental Transformation," *Administrative Science Quarterly* 37, no. 1 (1992): 48.

5   Peter M. Senge, *The Fifth Discipline: The Art and Practice of the Learning Organization* (London: Century Business, 1991); and William Edwards Deming, *Out of the Crisis* (Cambridge, MA: MIT Press, 2000).

6   Deming, *Out of the Crisis*, 24.

MODULE 3
THE PROBLEM

KEY POINTS

- Academics in the 1990s were concerned with the content, context, and process of organizational change.

- Other models of change proposed at the time are similar to those in *Leading Change*, but they emphasize different aspects of the change process.

- Kotter may well have been aware of the work of others operating in the same area, but he makes no direct reference to it.

Core Question

When John P. Kotter published *Leading Change* in the 1990s, organizational change was an active area of debate, largely due to the rapidly changing business environment resulting from globalization.* Authors at the time were writing about organizational change based around three themes:[1]

- Content: attempting to define common factors in both successful and unsuccessful change efforts (see, for example, W. Warner Burke* and George Litwin's* model and Thomas Vollman).*[2]

- Context: examining forces and conditions in the internal and external environment of organizations to see how they affect the change process (see, for example, Nils Finstad* and Heather Haveman).*[3]

- Process: focusing on the actual actions undertaken while initiating change at the level of external environment, firm, and individual (see, for example, Kurt Lewin,* Timothy Galpin,* Achilles A. Armenakis*).[4] Particular emphasis was

> ❝ It has been said that arguing against globalization is like arguing against the laws of gravity. ❞
>
> *The Globalist,* "Kofi Annan on Global Futures"

placed on how to *improve* change processes, rather than just *understand* them.

Kotter's work in *Leading Change* relates to the third theme. He defines different stages in the process of implementing change in organizations, with a series of actions that can be taken at the individual and firm level. Kotter was asking a core question: what factors hold back change efforts in large organizations, and what steps can be taken to improve organizations' ability to implement these efforts? It is important to understand the meaning of "change" in this context. By "change," Kotter means "restructuring, re-engineering, re-strategizing, acquisitions, downsizing, quality programs, and cultural renewal."[5] In other words, he is referring to any modification to the function or structure of the business. Kotter was not unique in asking this question. The originality of his argument lies in the broad sweep of his analysis and his ability to make it relevant to both academics and business people.

The Participants

Two scholars, whose work in the 1990s most resembles Kotter's, are Arnold Judson* and Timothy Galpin. Judson developed a model for implementing change that consists of five phases:

1. Analyze and plan the change.
2. Communicate the change.
3. Gain acceptance for new behaviors.
4. Change from the status quo to the desired state.
5. Consolidate the new state.[6]

A key element of Judson's model was to offer reward programs and incentives to minimize resistance from reluctant managers. Such ideas are absent from Kotter's model.

Galpin offered another model to guide implementation of the change process.[7] Rather than a series of key stages, he imagined a wheel made of nine wedges. The wedges of the model were:

1. Establish the need to change.
2. Develop and share a vision of that change.
3. Analyze the current situation.
4. Generate recommendations.
5. Detail the recommendations.
6. Pilot-test the recommendations.
7. Prepare the recommendations for rollout.
8. Roll out recommendations.
9. Measure, reinforce, and refine change.

Galpin's model is similar to Kotter's. Indeed, there are similarities between all three models; but while all end with building the change effort into the corporate culture,* there are clear differences in emphasis.

The Contemporary Debate
Although Kotter may have been aware of other authors writing on organizational change in the 1990s, *Leading Change*, like the *Harvard Business School* article it is based on, makes no direct reference to the work of others in the field. In fact, Kotter constructs his argument exclusively from his own experiences and intuition—there are no references provided. Unlike his predecessors, Kotter developed a comprehensive account of the entire change process from start to finish.

Rather than referring to other scholarly works, Kotter introduces *Leading Change* as an extension of the ideas he presented in his previous publications, including *A Force for Change: How Leadership Differs from Management*, and *Corporate Culture and Performance*.[8] As he writes in the preface: "Unlike my previous books, *Leading Change* is not filled with footnotes or endnotes. I have neither drawn examples or major ideas from any published source except my own writing nor tried to cite evidence from other sources to bolster my conclusions."[9] It is possible that this decision set *Leading Change* apart from other similar books of the period.

NOTES

1   Achilles A. Armenakis and Arthur G. Bedeian, "Organizational Change: A Review of Theory and Research in the 1990s," *Journal of Management* 25 (1999): 293–315.

2   See W. Warner Burke and George H. Litwin, "A Causal Model of Organizational Performance and Change," *Journal of Management* 18, no. 3 (1992): 523–45; and Thomas E. Vollmann, *The Transformation Imperative: Achieving Market Dominance Through Radical Change* (Boston: Harvard Business School Press, 1996).

3   Nils Finstad, "The Rhetoric of Organizational Change," *Human Relations* 51, no. 6 (1998): 717–40; and Heather A. Haveman, "Between a Rock and a Hard Place: Organizational Change and Performance Under Conditions of Fundamental Environmental Transformation," *Administrative Science Quarterly* 37, no. 1 (1992): 48–75.

4   Kurt Lewin, "Frontiers in Group Dynamics II: Channels of Group Life; Social Planning and Action Research," *Human Relations* 1 (1947): 143–53; Timothy J. Galpin, *The Human Side of Change: A Practical Guide to Organization Redesign* (San Francisco: Jossey-Bass Publishers, 1996); and Achilles A. Armenakis, Stanley G. Harris, and Hubert S. Feild, "Paradigms in Organizational Change: Change Agent and Change Target Perspectives," *Public Administration and Public Policy* 87 (2001): 631–58.

5   John P. Kotter, *Leading Change* (Boston: Harvard Business School Press, 1996), ix.

6   Arnold S. Judson, *Changing Behavior in Organizations: Minimizing Resistance to Change* (Cambridge, MA: Blackwell, 1991).

7   Galpin, *The Human Side of Change*.

8   John P. Kotter, *A Force for Change: How Leadership Differs from Management* (New York: Free Press, 1990); and John P. Kotter and James L. Heskett, *Corporate Culture and Performance* (New York: Free Press, 1992).

9   Kotter, *Leading Change*, x.

MODULE 4
THE AUTHOR'S CONTRIBUTION

KEY POINTS

- *Leading Change* is an expansion of a *Harvard Business Review* article that appeared in 1995, in which John Kotter laid out an eight-stage process for carrying out change in organizations.

- Kotter follows a simple formula in the book, first introducing a step to change, then illustrating it with an example, and elaborating on it through discussion.

- *Leading Change* largely builds on Kotter's previous work, though existing works on change from writers such as Chris Argyris* and Douglas McGregor* operate in similar areas.

Author's Aims

John P. Kotter's main aim in writing *Leading Change* was to expand on the ideas he presented in his 1995 *Harvard Business Review* article "Leading Change: Why Transformation Efforts Fail."[1] The article was well received, jumping to first place among reprints sold. The response Kotter had from readers inspired him to write more about the topic: "First, managers read the list of mistakes organizations often make when trying to effect real change and said *Yes! This is why we have achieved less than we hoped.* Second, readers found the eight-stage framework compelling."[2] In order to expand on the article, Kotter included "dozens and dozens of examples of what seems to work and what doesn't."[3] These additions not only made the book more interesting, but also clarified the vision behind Kotter's ideas and made his argument more credible.

❝ In the summer of 1994, I wrote an article for the *Harvard Business Review* entitled 'Leading Change: Why Transformation Efforts Fail.' It was based on my analysis of dozens of initiatives over the prior 15 years to produce significant useful change in organizations ... Even as I was finishing that piece I knew I wanted to write more on the subject, so I began this book shortly thereafter. ❞

John Kotter, *Leading Change*

In the full-length book, Kotter was able to do what he had envisaged, and the road map to change appears both feasible and practical. The book appeals primarily to senior managers, as it prepares them for the process of change, which can often be daunting without experience or guidance. Employees may find the book less relevant to their own experience, as the steps Kotter describes unfold in a top-down manner. Indeed, most of the responsibility for implementing change in Kotter's model is given to leaders in the organization, not to those lower in the corporate structure. The book's continued popularity, however, demonstrates that it remains core reading for managers and that the examples included were both appropriate and realistic.

Approach

Apart from the introductory and closing sections, *Leading Change* follows a simple formula: introduce one of the steps to change, and elaborate on that step with examples and general discussion. The book consists of relatively simple ideas presented in a straightforward manner. Kotter uses examples that will endear managers to his way of thinking. In fact, the purpose of many of the examples seems to be to give readers a reference point. Consider this example of meetings at a global pharmaceuticals company suffering from lagging sales: "Visit a typical management* meeting at the company and you begin to wonder if all the facts you gathered about the firm's revenues, income, stock price, customer complaints, competitive situation, and morale could have been wrong … The pace is often leisurely. The issues being discussed can be of marginal importance."[4] Most of Kotter's readers will have had involvement with complacent organizations. His aim with this example is clearly to build trust with the readers, and connect his ideas to their own experience.

Contribution in Context

Leading Change follows the same framework that was introduced in Kotter's original article, but with a more detailed discussion and numerous examples. Kotter had written many books on organizational change and leadership* before *Leading Change*, and his key ideas can be traced back to his earlier works, including *A Force for Change: How Leadership Differs from Management* and *Corporate Culture and Performance*. These two works, and his later book *The New Rules*,[5] contain similar ideas to *Leading Change* and are still in print. To some extent the best reference point for how Kotter's ideas have evolved is his own previous writing on change and transformation.

Earlier works on change management focused on aspects such as managers' actions or behavior, not with change as a step-by-step process. Two notable examples are Chris Argyris's books on how senior managers behave in difficult situations and Douglas McGregor's *The Human Side of Enterprise*, which identifies factors and forces that can create a positive environment for employees' performance.[6] These writers form a background to Kotter's work, but *Leading Change* itself largely exists outside the academic tradition on change.

NOTES

1   John P. Kotter, "Leading Change: Why Transformation Efforts Fail," *Harvard Business Review* 73, no. 2 (1995): 59–67.

2   John P. Kotter, *Leading Change* (Boston: Harvard Business School Press, 1996), ix.

3   Kotter, *Leading Change*, ix.

4   Kotter, *Leading Change*, 37.

5   John P. Kotter, *A Force for Change: How Leadership Differs from Management* (New York: Free Press, 1990); John P. Kotter and James L. Heskett, *Corporate Culture and Performance* (New York: Free Press, 1992); John P. Kotter, *The New Rules: Eight Business Breakthroughs to Career Success in the 21st Century* (New York: Free Press, 1997).

6   Chris Argyris, *Interpersonal Competence and Organizational Effectiveness* (Homewood, IL: Dorsey Press, 1962); Chris Argyris, *Organization and Innovation* (Homewood, IL: R. D. Irwin, 1965); and Douglas McGregor and Joel Cutcher-Gershenfeld, *The Human Side of Enterprise* (New York: McGraw-Hill, 2006).

SECTION 2
IDEAS

MODULE 5
MAIN IDEAS

KEY POINTS

- John Kotter's *Leading Change* focuses on how business organizations can evolve and the rise of globalization.*

- Kotter lists eight common mistakes organizations make when attempting change and offers an eight-step change process.

- Kotter presents his ideas simply, with minimal jargon, and with reference to several examples.

Key Themes

John P. Kotter's *Leading Change* revolves around the theme of how business organizations can evolve and transform. The word "change" appears throughout the book, and has many meanings. As examples of change, Kotter imagines a business being forced to "reduce costs, improve the quality of products and services, locate new opportunities for growth, and increase productivity"—though this list is likely incomplete.[1] Kotter associates change with any introduction of new business practices in response to changes in the external business environment. Importantly, his steps for implementing change apply to whatever change or challenge faces the business, whether it's an accounting shift or a new manufacturing procedure. The steps should apply equally well to a pharmaceutical company, an oil company, or a large university.

A second theme, which is closely related to the first, is the necessity of change due to globalization—the transformation of trade regulations* and transport costs that have led to markets reaching well beyond their physical boundaries. For Kotter, globalization is the reason for many of the change initiatives described in the book. As he

❝ To some degree, the downside of change is inevitable. Whenever human communities are forced to adjust to shifting conditions, pain is ever present. But a significant amount of the waste and anguish we've witnessed in the past decade *is* avoidable. ❞

John Kotter, *Leading Change*

writes: "A globalized economy is creating more opportunities for everyone, forcing firms to make dramatic improvements not only to compete and prosper but also to merely survive."[2] In other words, whereas before globalization change was desirable, in a global economy it is *vital* for survival.

Exploring the Ideas

Leading Change addresses the key theme of organizational change by developing a roadmap for managers to follow as they implement change in their organizations. The text has two main components: a list of common errors and mistakes made by managers, and an eight-stage change process.

Based on Kotter's analysis of change initiatives in the corporate world, he identifies eight common errors that managers make while implementing change. These are as follows:

1. Changing organizations without creating a sense of urgency among the employees—in other words, "allowing too much complacency."[3] If employees do not feel a need to change their own behavior, they will not understand the seriousness of the situation or help the change process.
2. Managers failing to create a guiding coalition* with key members of the organization. While change efforts may survive for a while without a powerful coalition, "sooner or later, countervailing forces undermine the initiatives."[4]

3. Lack of a sensible vision.

4. Miscommunication, under-communication, or lack of communication.

5. Failing to create an enabling environment. Organizations sometimes fail to change because of obstacles such as a rigid "organizational structure," including "supervisors who refuse to adapt to new circumstances."[5]

6. Failing to create short-term wins,* such as "money-saving course corrections" (or small reforms) or partial implementation of new production methods that help build momentum for the larger change effort.[6]

7. Declaring victory before the change process is complete.

8. New behaviors not being rooted deeply enough in the corporate culture,* so that changes are not anchored properly for continued success.[7]

Kotter's solution to these problems is his sequential eight-stage process. A manager may go through multiple stages at the same time, but Kotter warns that skipping any of the steps, or not giving them sufficient attention, will hurt the change process, which will not "build and develop in a natural way."[8] The process is as follows:

1. Establish a sense of urgency.

2. Create the guiding coalition.

3. Develop a vision and strategy.

4. Communicate the change vision.

5. Empower broad-based action.

6. Generate short-term wins.

7. Consolidate gains and produce more change.

8. Anchor new approaches in the corporate culture.[9]

Each of the steps is discussed in detail in *Leading Change*, with a separate chapter dedicated to each, featuring advice on implementation supported by examples from different companies. For example, in step 3, vision refers to "a picture of the future with some implicit or explicit commentary on why people should strive to create that future."[10] One of the examples Kotter uses to show the importance of vision is a "medium-size retail business." An executive of this company introduced a promising plan that was challenged for being "too fuzzy and soft."[11] In spite of this opposition, the executive was able to successfully implement his vision by relying on the first two steps in the change process: building coalitions and establishing a sense of urgency.

Language and Expression

Kotter expresses his ideas in a very simple, non-academic, and comprehensible style using practical examples. The placement and content of these examples are crucial for understanding his ideas. For example, in a chapter about complacency, Kotter introduces a case study of a "major global pharmaceuticals company" that "has had more than its share of challenges over the past few years."[12] Citing conversations with employees, Kotter observes that the employees are aware of a problem, but: "The energy level is rarely high."[13] Well-placed examples like this, based on real-life situations, make the author's propositions more convincing and easier to relate to.

Leading Change is mostly free of business and economic jargon. Even readers with only a limited experience of management* or corporate culture should easily understand each of the eight change strategies. When Kotter uses business language such as "short term wins,"* "corporate culture," or "new vision," he presents the ideas in a way that does not require specific knowledge. This makes his text accessible to a very wide audience.

NOTES

1   John P. Kotter, *Leading Change* (Boston: Harvard Business School Press, 1996), 3.

2   Kotter, *Leading Change*, 18.

3   Kotter, *Leading Change*, 4.

4   Kotter, *Leading Change*, 6.

5   Kotter, *Leading Change*, 10.

6   Kotter, *Leading Change*, 12.

7   Kotter, *Leading Change*, 4–15.

8   Kotter, *Leading Change*, 24.

9   Kotter, *Leading Change*, 20–2.

10   Kotter, *Leading Change*, 68.

11   Kotter, *Leading Change*, 80.

12   Kotter, *Leading Change*, 36.

13   Kotter, *Leading Change*, 36.

SECONDARY IDEAS

KEY POINTS

- John Kotter's secondary ideas include: the differences between leadership* and management;* characteristics of the organization of the future; and characteristics of lifelong learners.*

- Kotter emphasizes the importance of urgency and a lack of complacency in organizations of the future.

- Kotter's discussion of globalization* as a coming force is less important today as it is now already a fact of business life.

Other Ideas

An important secondary idea in John P. Kotter's *Leading Change* is the role and importance of leadership in carrying out change. Kotter differentiates between management and leadership, and believes managers must adopt the characteristics of leaders to change and transform their firms successfully. He associates management with stagnant bureaucracies and effective leadership with transformative organizations:* "With a strong emphasis on management but not leadership, bureaucracy and an inward focus take over. But with continued success, the result mostly of market dominance, the problem often goes unaddressed and an unhealthy arrogance begins to evolve. All these characteristics then make any transformation effort much more difficult."[1]

Kotter does not dismiss management skills entirely, and argues that effective management is required for the important tasks of planning, budgeting, organizing, staffing, and problem solving. In contrast,

> **" Major transformations are often associated with one highly visible individual ... This is a very dangerous belief. "**
> John Kotter, *Leading Change*

leadership is the process that helps organizations form and then adapt to significant changes in the environment. According to Kotter: "Successful transformation is 70 to 90 percent leadership and only 10 to 30 percent management."[2]

Two related ideas concern the characteristics of the "organization of the future" and how to develop the traits of successful leaders in a globalized economy.[3] Kotter argues that as rapid change becomes more important in the business environment, organizations must be able to maintain the following: a strong sense of urgency, effective teamwork among executives, good communication of vision, the empowerment of a broad base of employees, and an ability to change the company culture. Further, Kotter discusses the ideal executive of the future. Perhaps most importantly, he says that future leaders must be dedicated to "lifelong learning."

Exploring the Ideas

Referring to his argument that leadership is more valuable than management, Kotter argues that the problem is not so much about managing change, but that managers do not have sufficient leadership qualities. Managers in the traditional sense create an "overmanaged and underled" corporate culture of bureaucracy, arrogance, and insularity.[4] Rather than removing management altogether, Kotter suggests finding and developing managers who have leadership qualities.

In the final chapters of the book, Kotter looks to the future. In a chapter entitled, "The Organization of the Future," he describes what he believes will be the keys to managerial success in the future, assuming the rate of change in the business environment continues. One of the most important characteristics of these organizations, Kotter says, is maintaining a sense of urgency. He writes: "A higher rate of urgency does not imply ever present panic, anxiety, or fear. It means a state in which complacency is virtually absent, in which people are always looking for both problems and opportunities, and in which the norm is 'do it now.'"[5] This urgency is closely related to another of Kotter's predictions: broad-based empowerment.* Citing several technology companies that have successfully created a culture of empowerment, Kotter says that in organizations that deal with a high level of change, you will find "unusually flat hierarchies, little bureaucracy, a propensity for risk-taking, workforces that largely manage themselves, and senior-level people who focus on providing leadership."[6] In other words, in successful organizations of the future, meddling management will be replaced by empowered employees and executives focused on leadership.

In order to ensure that organizations can find suitable employees for these roles, Kotter describes his ideal future leader: the lifelong learner. According to Kotter, lifelong learners are defined by five characteristics: a willingness to take risks, honest self-assessment, aggressive collection of the opinions of others, careful listening, and openness to new ideas.[7] He argues it is more important to continue to learn over time than to excel at any given point in life.[8]

Overlooked

The core ideas of *Leading Change* are easy to digest and therefore little has been overlooked. Naturally, the eight-stage process has been the most widely cited feature of the book, and less attention has been given to Kotter's secondary ideas. In the two chapters where Kotter looks beyond the eight-stage process to the future of organizations and leaders, he is careful to manage expectations. "Speculating on the future is always hazardous," he notes, "but the discussion presented in this book has rather clear implications."[9] The areas where Kotter is less sure of his arguments have been less widely circulated and shared by readers. However, the list-like nature of Kotter's main argument has made that argument easy to share as a standalone entity separate from the book itself.

It is true that Kotter's discussion of globalization in *Leading Change* has declined in importance. When he wrote the book in the 1990s, the prospect of widespread global markets was relatively new; in the twenty-first century it is commonplace. It is therefore unlikely that an executive today would use Kotter's book to highlight the many challenges created by global markets. Globalization is now a given, not an emerging phenomenon requiring special thought or preparation.

NOTES

1   John P. Kotter, *Leading Change* (Boston: Harvard Business School Press, 1996), 27.

2   Kotter, *Leading Change*, 26.

3   Kotter, *Leading Change*, 161.

4   Kotter, *Leading Change*, 43.

5   Kotter, *Leading Change*, 162.

6   Kotter, *Leading Change*, 167.

7   Kotter, *Leading Change*, 183.

8   Kotter, *Leading Change*, 181.

9   Kotter, *Leading Change*, 162.

ACHIEVEMENT

KEY POINTS

- In *Leading Change*, John Kotter was successful in expanding on his ideas about how change in business could happen most effectively.

- The book has proved to be useful in areas outside of business, including war studies and health service research.

- *Leading Change* would benefit from a broader cultural and geographic perspective. The book's focus is purely American.

Assessing the Argument

John P. Kotter's intention with *Leading Change* was to expand on the ideas presented in his earlier article of the same name, and in this he was successful. Though there were other change models in the 1990s, Kotter's is unique in focusing specifically on the *process* of change and in his practical style of presentation. While others were more overtly academic in their discussion of change, Kotter maintained a close eye on the business world. The examples he uses make his model compelling.

Despite this success, Kotter's change model is not universal. His work is based solely on examples from the Western world. Organizations in the developing world and fragile states face far more turbulent and volatile environments. They are more vulnerable to natural disasters and to uncertainty in their political and technological environment. The context, environment, and macroeconomic* environment that create change will be different and may require a different framework for change management.

> ❝ Comparing today's business environment to 20 years ago, it strikes me that wins—and an intentional approach to producing them—have only increased in importance as the fuel of large-scale sustainable change. The energy they produce can overpower the effects of speed, distraction, and dilution that conspire against change efforts. They can help break down change-blocking silos. So, too, the complexity of globalization, which increasingly feels like a high-speed game of 3-D chess. ❞
>
> Gregg LeStage, "How Have Kotter's Eight Steps for Change Changed?"

Another important contextual factor at the time the text was written was the North American Free Trade Agreement (NAFTA),* established in 1994, which opened free trade* between the United States, Canada, and Mexico. This meant increased competition and greater challenges for firms, which had to change and transform their business processes so they did not lose market share. It is likely that NAFTA contributed to the popularity of *Leading Change*, as managers had to plan for a more integrated world economy.

Achievement in Context

Leading Change has not only gained acclaim and recognition in the field of business and management,* but has also been used by academics and practitioners in other social science disciplines. Its eight-stage model provides a road map for managers of all kinds and has been used in war studies, health services research, information and technology (IT) management, industrial relations, and much more. Case studies have been designed around the model to teach students about leading change efforts. The work's academic application has proved extremely useful for researchers and scholars. Studies in health services research have used Kotter's framework to reform the state-level health services in the United Kingdom. IT management specialists have used it to explain the introduction of new technology in organizations and to minimize resistance among workers confronting new structures, processes, and machinery.

Although *Leading Change* is based on examples from the private sector and corporate world, the model has been widely used to explain change and public service reform across various social sectors such as health services and education. Its universal appeal is also evident in its academic application across various fields in the social sciences. This wide application of Kotter's work may have surprised him, as the book was initially intended primarily for senior management and practitioners in the corporate sector.

Leading Change has also been important in management development workshops. Such workshops are now featured as a development opportunity in every organization. Kotter's model is sequential, has clear stages, and is targeted at senior management: it serves as an excellent tool to analyze complex situations.

Limitations

Kotter describes a general process of change, which should be applicable to almost all change situations. One of the biggest limitations of the book, however, is its lack of examples from the developing world. The author has mainly used examples from his own observations, derived from his experience with organizations in North America, and he focuses on a sample of firms that are mainly from one country: the United States. The eight-stage framework can still be applied universally, and the steps and propositions are reasonably generic. Nevertheless, managers are advised to keep both the internal and external environment in mind while making an organizational analysis.

Context is another limitation. Organizational change and transformation is no longer a "one-time" activity as it may have been in the mid-1990s. It is now more of a permanent feature, as firms continuously change and transform to maintain their competitive edge. The importance of context, especially geographical context, cannot be ignored, but Kotter does not focus on national differences. Change is also no longer only an American or North American phenomenon; as business becomes global, organizations must predict and respond to change around the world and manage it in tandem. A comparative analysis including evidence from other parts of the world would greatly improve Kotter's original analysis.

MODULE 8
PLACE IN THE AUTHOR'S WORK

KEY POINTS

- John Kotter's career has been consistently concerned with the analysis and implementation of change efforts in organizations; he has carried out these efforts both as a scholar and as a management consultant.*

- Kotter defines his own career in two stages, the first stage was based around research, the second around implementation.

- *Leading Change* is one of Kotter's most important books, but he had already built a significant reputation before its publication in 1996.

Positioning

John P. Kotter wrote *Leading Change* after already writing several books and articles on change and leadership.* In his 1979 article, "Choosing Strategies for Change," co-authored with Leonard Schlesinger,* Kotter introduced many of the ideas that would later appear in *Leading Change*. He and Schlesinger highlight the importance of recognizing "people's limited tolerance for change"[1] as a key resistance factor. This observation is closely related to the sense of urgency Kotter describes in *Leading Change*. In *A Force for Change: How Leadership Differs from Management*, published in 1990, Kotter is mostly concerned with the role of effective leadership in change efforts. The distinction between leadership and management,* a key feature of *Leading Change*, appears throughout that book too: "leadership and management differ in terms of their primary function. The first can produce useful change, the second can produce orderly results which keep something working efficiently."[2]

> **❝** Up until this project, all of my past work, research now spanning many decades, has used the same formula. Find cases representing the highest 10% or 20% of performers. Observe what they do. Talk to people who have lived in those situations. Then do the same for the average performers and the laggards. Look for patterns that show the differences. Report those factors with an emphasis on factors that you can change—to take average performance to high or lagging results at least up to the norm. **❞**
>
> John Kotter, *Accelerate: Building Strategic Agility for a Faster-Moving World*

The most direct forerunner to *Leading Change*, however, was Kotter's 1995 article "Leading Change: Why Transformation Efforts Fail."[3] This article provided the first instance of Kotter's eight steps for carrying out change. Since the publication of *Leading Change*, Kotter has refined his ideas in several books and articles, most notably *Our Iceberg is Melting*, published in 2006. That book tells the story of a group of penguins stranded on a melting iceberg and the importance of creating a sense of urgency to save themselves. Again this is a theme that is prominent in *Leading Change* and earlier Kotter works.

Integration

Kotter divides his career into two phases: a research phase, which took place from 1972 to 2008, and an implementation phase from 2008 onward.[4] The research phase is dominated by the development of the eight-stage process for carrying out change that is detailed in *Leading Change*. Kotter's work has almost exclusively focused on how organizations behave in times of transformation. As such, his work has covered topics including leadership, management, risk taking, and organizational behavior.* The theme of managing change is ever present in his writing, if sometimes only on a background level.

The implementation phase of Kotter's career is mostly defined by his work at Kotter International, the consulting firm he co-founded in 2008. Kotter International's mission statement is closely tied to the themes of Kotter's research, specifically *Leading Change*. The eight-stage process features prominently on the Kotter International website. For instance, there is a blog post on the website written by Gregg LeStage,* entitled "Is your organization developing change managers or change leaders?" In the blog, LeStage emphasizes the distinction between management and leadership: "The difference between a change manager and a change leader—as noted in the definitions above—is significant. Change managers typically drive incremental change, ensuring work is done on time and within budget. Change leaders, on the other hand, are less adverse to getting 'messy' and taking risks, influencing and inspiring behaviors that lead to large-scale transformation."[5] The similarity between the tone and content of the Kotter International website and *Leading Change* suggests a high degree of integration of Kotter's work throughout his career.

Significance

Leading Change is among Kotter's most influential works. The Kotter International website emphasizes the book's importance: "For 40 years, Harvard Business School Professor John Kotter has engaged in broad and deep studies investigating why 70% of businesses fail to execute their strategies and only 5% meet or exceed them … Chief among [Kotter's] successes was the development of the award-winning 8-Step Process for Leading Change in 1996."[6] *Leading Change* is also one of Kotter's best-selling books, and was selected in 2011 as one of the 25 most influential management books by *Time Magazine*.[7]

Leading Change remains one of Kotter's major works, but it would be an overstatement to say Kotter built his reputation on the book. Prior to its publication, he was already a well-recognized figure in business scholarship and had held a prominent position at Harvard

Business School for more than two decades. Also, *Leading Change* is by no means Kotter's most academic or rigorous book; it includes no footnotes or references to other writers. The book is best viewed as a distillation of Kotter's thinking up to the mid-1990s and one of the foundations on which he built his subsequent work.

NOTES

1   John Kotter and Leonard Schlesinger, "Choosing Strategies for Change," *Harvard Business Review* (2008 reprint), accessed May 21, 2015, https://hbr.org/2008/07/choosing-strategies-for-change/ar/1.

2   John P. Kotter, *A Force for Change: How Leadership Differs from Management* (New York: Free Press, 1990), 7.

3   John P. Kotter, "Leading Change: Why Transformation Efforts Fail," *Harvard Business Review* 73, no. 2 (1995): 59–67.

4   "About Us," Kotter International, accessed May 21, 2015, http://www.kotterinternational.com/about-us/.

5   Gregg LeStage, "Is your organization developing change managers or change leaders?" accessed May 21, 2015, http://www.kotterinternational.com/insights/organization-developing-change-managers-change-leaders/.

6   Kotter International, "About Us."

7   "The 25 Most Influential Business Management Books," *Time Magazine*, August 9, 2011, accessed May 21, 2015, http://content.time.com/time/specials/packages/article/0,28804,2086680_2086683_2087679,00.html.

SECTION 3
IMPACT

MODULE 9
THE FIRST RESPONSES

KEY POINTS

- *Leading Change* has been criticized for being too rigid and for placing too much emphasis on top-down leadership.*

- While Kotter has had minimal interaction with his critics, he made a significant modification to the model in 2012 to account for a more flexible business environment.

- Critics of *Leading Change* have noted that a changing business world has required alterations to Kotter's model.

Criticism

One of the criticisms of John P. Kotter's work in *Leading Change* is that, given the complexity of the change process, no one model can be entirely effective. Kotter's book has been immensely popular: so if his model is correct, the success rate of change efforts in large organizations should have increased; but this does not seem to have been the case. As Carolyn Aiken and Scott Keller write: "Kotter's research revealed that only 30 percent of change programs succeed. Since the book's release, literally thousands of books and journal articles have been published on the topic, and courses dedicated to managing change are now part of many major MBA* (Master of Business Administration) programs. Yet in 2008, a McKinsey* survey of 3,199 executives around the world found, as Kotter did, that only one transformation in three succeeds. Other studies over the past 10 years reveal remarkably similar results. It seems that, despite prolific output, the field of change management hasn't led to more successful change programs."[1]

With this in mind, Aiken and Keller suggest that the practice of change management is "in need of a transformation through an

> ❝ Even though it is difficult to identify any consensus regarding a framework for organizational change management, there seems to be an agreement on two important issues. Firstly, it is agreed that the pace of change has never been greater than in the current business environment ... Secondly, there is a consensus that change, being triggered by internal or external factors, comes in all shapes, forms, and sizes. ❞
>
> Rune Todnem By, *Organizational Change Management: A Critical Review*

improved understanding of how humans interpret their environment and choose to act."[2] In other words, rigid models such as Kotter's may only be of limited effect.

Another criticism of the book concerns Kotter's description of change as a top-down practice. In his 2009 article "Rebuilding Companies as Communities," Henry Mintzberg* concedes that "Kotter's approach sounds sensible enough and has probably worked," but challenges the focus on a "driving leader" to bring about change. He writes: "Perhaps it's time to rebuild companies not from the top down or even the bottom up but from the middle out—through groups of middle managers who bond together and drive key changes in their organization."[3] Although Kotter mentioned the need to create short-term wins* for employees, top-down change can lead to frustration among employees. Further, the sequential, step-by-step nature of Kotter's model does not take into account the many unexpected problems that might have to be dealt with for a change effort to succeed.

Some writers have challenged Kotter's views on management* and leadership. Gary Yukl,* a management theorist, has argued that leadership is part of the managerial tasks that every manager must undertake in an organization and that leadership and management skills are equally important to run and transform organizations successfully.[4]

Responses

Kotter has had little public interaction with his critics, though he has since revised his eight-step *Leading Change* model. In his article, "Accelerate!" published in the *Harvard Business Review* in 2012,[5] Kotter replaced the model with a "strategy system" that "expands on the eight-step method I first documented 15 years ago."[6] There are three main differences between the eight-step model and the strategic model. First, the step model was "often used in rigid, finite, and sequential ways," whereas the strategy model recognizes factors that accelerate change, which are "concurrent and always at work."[7] This modification may have been inspired by changing circumstances in the business environment—as the rate of change has increased, maintaining a linear, step-by-step progression has become impossible. Second, the step process was led by a "small, powerful group," while "accelerators pull in as many people as possible from throughout the organization to form a 'volunteer army.'"[8] Finally, the accelerator framework is built around a view of the organization that is informed by social networks, rather than as a top-down structure.

While Kotter does not cite critics of his work as inspirations for these changes, he references three scholars whose work led him in this direction: Michael Porter,* a professor at Harvard Business School, who provided Kotter with the "wake-up call that organizations need to pay attention to strategy much more explicitly and frequently;"[9] Clayton Christensen,* also of Harvard, whose work showed him how poorly organizations manage technological change* in a fast-paced environment; and Daniel Kahneman,* who referred to "the brain as two coordinated systems, one more emotional and one more rational."[10] It is notable that none of these scholars focus on organizational change in particular.

Conflict and Consensus

As the business environment is complex and constantly changing, no single model of transformation and change can be definitive. Some trends in the literature being produced on the subject, however, as well as Kotter's own alterations to his model, suggest a degree of consensus. Part of that consensus is that change models must incorporate new methods, such as social network analysis:* this can give a more accurate picture of how information is transmitted through an organization than the official company structure might suggest. Such tools were only partially developed in 1996, so it is not surprising that Kotter's original book did not make use of them. Another part of this general consensus is that organizational change is unlikely to unfold as a sequence of events and instead is constantly evolving and chaotic. As Leandro Herrero* writes in a 2014 review of *Leading Change*: "The linear, sequential world has gone."[11] Herrero intended this as a critique of Kotter's model, but Kotter himself had already disowned the sequential nature of his model.

Another aspect of consensus around the themes in *Leading Change* is that transformation is an integral part of today's business environment, and that organizations should dedicate resources to understanding how they can most effectively transform. When Kotter wrote the book in 1996, he had to spend considerable time convincing his audience that managing globalization* would require more focused attention on change efforts. This is no longer required, as globalization has been fully integrated into the business environment.

NOTES

1   Carolyn Aiken and Scott Keller, "The Irrational Side of Change Management," April 2009, accessed May 21, 2015, http://www.mckinsey.com/insights/organization/the_irrational_side_of_change_management.

2   Aiken and Keller, "The Irrational Side of Change Management."

3   Henry Mintzberg, "Rebuilding Companies as Communities," *Harvard Business Review*, July 2009, accessed May 21, 2015, https://hbr.org/2009/07/rebuilding-companies-as-communities.

4   Gary A. Yukl, *Leadership in Organizations* (Upper Saddle River, NJ: Prentice Hall, 2010).

5   John P. Kotter, "Accelerate!" *Harvard Business Review*, November 2012, accessed May 21, 2015, https://hbr.org/2012/11/accelerate.

6   Kotter, "Accelerate!"

7   Kotter, "Accelerate!"

8   Kotter, "Accelerate!"

9   Kotter, "Accelerate!"

10 Kotter, "Accelerate!"

11 Leandro Herrero, "John Kotter's 8 Step Change Management model is the best change model of the last Century. Why this is still alive in 2014 is beyond me," October 21, 2014, accessed May 21, 2015, http://leandroherrero.com/john-kotters-8-step-change-management-model-is-the-best-change-model-of-the-last-century-why-this-is-still-alive-in-2014-is-beyond-me/.

MODULE 10
THE EVOLVING DEBATE

KEY POINTS

- *Leading Change* was one of the first models of the process of organizational change, and inspired later work in the field.

- Change research is categorized in three ways: by the rate of occurrence, by how it comes about, and by scale. *Leading Change* is in the second category.

- *Leading Change* has been highly influential and helped inspire other models from scholars such as Peter Senge,* Jeffrey Liker,* and James Franz,* whose work examines change processes in a wider set of circumstances.

Uses and Problems

When John P. Kotter's *Leading Change* was first published in 1996, many authors already saw change as an inevitable part of the business environment. As time passed, it was recognized that change should be a permanent feature of all organizational strategies, and more people started developing their own change process models. This ever-growing literature emphasized the importance of change and how it could be approached, but gave little observed data to prove the theories and models that were presented.

Leading Change was written at a time when organizations were approaching business transformation in terms of reengineering,* total quality management,* reorganization, and technological change.* The popularity of Kotter's article had already shown that people were thinking about organizational change, but were unclear how to approach it to get the best results. The publication of the book marked

> **❝** Just as organizations are going to be forced to learn, change, and constantly reinvent themselves in the twenty-first century, so will increasing numbers of individuals. [Kotter] goes on to say that as the rate of change increases, the willingness and ability to keep developing, that is to keep learning, become central to career success for individuals and to economic success for organizations. **❞**
>
> Gary Tomlinson, "Book Review on 'Leading Change' by John Kotter"

the beginning of *process* models of organizational change: Kotter made the process less mysterious and less unpredictable. He showed that the results of change could be foreseen and that his model, if followed correctly and in sequence, could lead to successful organizational transformation.

Later works by authors such as Peter Senge, Jeffrey K. Liker, and James K. Franz developed Kotter's ideas so they could be applied to a wider range of circumstances. Their work focused on the theme of organizational change under chaotic and complex conditions. They took into consideration contingency factors* (unknown influences or events) and environments (both internal and external) that force organizations to change and adapt. Because such forces cannot be planned for, the change effort cannot be described in a step-by-step, sequential manner: the authors therefore propose the idea of *cyclical** change.

Schools of Thought

Change literature can be categorized into three main streams or schools of thought:[1]

- Change characterized by the *rate* of occurrence.
- Change characterized by *how* it comes about.
- Change characterized by *scale*.

Kotter's work belongs to the second school, where change is dealt with by how it comes about. This school traces its roots to Kurt M. Lewin's* work. According to Lewin, a successful change initiative will pass through three stages: unfreezing the current stage; change, or moving to the new level; and refreezing the level.[2] This model proposes a planned approach to change and argues that we need to discard old behavior, structures, processes, and culture. Other notable authors who have worked on the planned approach and have developed similar models are Richard Luecke* and Bernard Burnes.* Burnes criticized the idea that there is one change strategy that is best, arguing that each model merely seeks to replace one set of prescriptions with another. He believed instead that organizations do have real choices in what they change and how they change it.[3]

The authors in this school of thought have mostly put forward planned, sequential models of change that are similar to Kotter's. Some have taken environmental factors into consideration and adapted their work to include contingency factors: things do not always go according to the plan and at times it becomes impossible to stick to the plan. Managers need to be cautious, deal with contingencies, and tailor their plans accordingly. Kotter's model of change serves as a benchmark for all subsequent models of change in this school of thought. Later developments in the field have proven that his model is a good starting point for managing change and transformation in organizations.

In Current Scholarship

Today, the topic of organizational change is an active area of debate and scholarship, though attention has moved from understanding the *process* of change as a sequence of steps to understanding change more broadly. Many of the major thinkers in this area have now moved on from Kotter's work as they apply new research systems to the change process. Kotter's ideas are probably best represented in the work of members of his own consulting firm, Kotter International. The firm publishes regular articles on change in a similar framework and tone to *Leading Change*. A recent piece, for example, written by Gregg LeStage,* asks, "Is your organization developing change managers or change leaders?" The article asks readers to choose between a set of options, such as: "We keep all projects on budget" or "We're actively mobilizing resources" to determine whether their organization is producing change leaders or change managers.[4] This distinction first appeared in *Leading Change* and continues to be an important part of Kotter's framework.

Another article discusses the question of whether or not leadership* can be taught, noting: "As Professor John Kotter has so often written, the most effective leaders know how and when to appeal to peoples' heads and hearts: it's all about balance. This is never so important as when change is the order of the day or year—or era."[5] Yet another piece discusses the decision of President Obama* to use the Internet show "Between Two Ferns" to advertise the changes to health care introduced by his Affordable Care Act* of 2010. The author connects the event to the techniques of successful communicators—an important theme in *Leading Change*—by concluding that "superior communicators must willingly deliver outside of their comfort zones."[6]

NOTES

1   Rune Todnem By, "Organizational Change Management: A Critical Review," *Journal of Change Management* 5 (2005): 369–80.

2   Kurt Lewin, "Frontiers in Group Dynamics II: Channels of Group Life; Social Planning and Action Research," *Human Relations* 1 (1947): 143–53.

3   Richard Luecke, *Managing Change and Transition* (Boston: Harvard Business School Press, 2003); and Bernard Burnes, "No Such Thing as … a 'One Best Way' to Manage Organizational Change," *Management Decision* 34, no. 10 (1996): 11–18.

4   Gregg LeStage, "Is your organization developing change managers or change leaders?" accessed May 21, 2015, http://www.kotterinternational.com/insights/organization-developing-change-managers-change-leaders/.

5   Gregg LeStage, "Can Leadership be Taught," accessed May 21, 2015, http://www.kotterinternational.com/insights/can-leadership-be-taught/.

6   Shaun Spearmon, "Why 'Between Two Ferns' Is Obama's Health Care Secret Weapon," accessed May 21, 2015, http://www.kotterinternational.com/insights/two-ferns-obamas-health-care-secret-weapon/.

MODULE 11
IMPACT AND INFLUENCE TODAY

KEY POINTS

- *Leading Change* is a seminal book in change management literature and continues to have an influence today.
- A debate continues regarding the differences and relative benefits and drawbacks of linear versus more complex change models.
- Some critics of Kotter's position challenge the rigidity of his model, suggesting that common sense and flexibility are more important than prescribed steps.

Position

John P. Kotter's *Leading Change* is a classic in the field of change management and continues to have an influence today. Much of the influence of the book, however, is channeled through Kotter's subsequent work, which has refined and revised aspects of his eight-step model for change.

There is no single formula for organizational transformation, but following a plan such as Kotter's eight-stage framework can increase the chances of successful organizational transformation. In his book on leadership* theory, Peter Northouse* acknowledges the importance of leadership in bringing about change, and suggests that management* and leadership are not only complementary, but integral to successful managers.[1] *Leading Change*'s value has been enhanced by such later works.

Change and transformation have affected all organizations for the last two to three decades. The concept of organizational change and transformation in the 1990s was not very different from what it is

66 Virtually all organizations on earth go through a very similar life cycle. They begin with a network-like structure, sort of like a solar system with a sun, planets, moons and even satellites. Founders are at the center. Others are at various nodes working on different initiatives. Action is opportunity seeking and risk taking, all guided by a vision that people buy into ... Over time, a successful organization evolves through a series of stages ... into an enterprise that is structured as a hierarchy and is driven by well-known managerial processes. 99

John Kotter, *Accelerate: Building Strategic Agility for a Faster-Moving World*

today. But change and transformation in organizations has become more complex. Despite more than two decades of research in organizational change and transformation, change still tends to be "reactive, discontinuous and ad hoc with a reported failure rate of around 70 percent of all change programs initiated."[2] The current debate still revolves around finding a suitable framework for organizational change management. Despite many authors coming up with change frameworks, the above figure shows that more work needs to be done. Kotter's book continues to play an important role in such research.

Interaction

Leading Change does not directly conflict with contemporary thinkers or schools of thought, but it does bring together the author's earlier ideas and works on the importance of leadership and change as a process. The last 20 years have seen a great deal of research around this theme, and there continue to be differences between linear change models and complex change models. Linear models suggest a step-by-step process—if managers in a company carry out each step in order, the initiative should be successful. In contrast, complex change models describe change as an ongoing and nonlinear process.

Despite this research and a number of articles and books on change management, most change initiatives still do not achieve their desired results.[3] This presents a challenge to theorists proposing change models—particularly models that have been put into practice such as Kotter's. The time is ripe to revisit the models and come up with new theories of change and transformation. Malcolm Higgs* and Deborah Rowland's* 2005 article[4] reports that in practice, change approaches based on complexity (for example the approaches of Peter Senge,* and Jeffrey K. Liker* and James K. Franz)*[5] rather than linearity (for example those of Kotter himself, and of Michael Hammer* and James Champy)*[6] have proven more successful.

The Continuing Debate

Change literature is a diverse area of research and debate. Kotter has modified his change model to adapt to current business conditions and now incorporates a more flexible approach based on recent research in the behavioral sciences. Some writers still challenge Kotter's model in its original form. The consultant Leandro Herrero* has criticized Kotter for continuing to promote his rigid, step-by-step change model, even though the complexity of the world has shown that greater flexibility is needed. He writes: "No revolution will ever be made with Kotter steps. Not the 1996, not the 2014 steps. Yet, maybe 'revolution' is not the target of industrial reinvention, so, no problems here. But, dare to ignore it. For great management, read Kotter, say thanks, and then look outside the window."[7]

Notably, this most recent criticism is of Kotter's 2014 rewrite of his change model, not the 1996 version presented in *Leading Change*. Herrero suggests Kotter's new, less linear model is still too rigid. As he says, mockingly referring to Kotter's own suggestion that managers carry out the steps "concurrently and continuously": "Welcome to 2014, or 2015. The 'run the steps concurrently and continuously' has taken around 19 years to materialize as a piece of advice, as his website says, 'after extensive research'. This non-accelerated discovery can only be matched by Vatican speed."[8] Criticisms such as this are rare, but express an alternative view that may be less visible due to the popularity and prestige of Kotter's work.

NOTES

1   Peter Guy Northouse, *Leadership: Theory and Practice* (Thousand Oaks, CA: Sage Publications, 2004).

2   Rune Todnem By, "Organisational Change Management: A Critical Review," *Journal of Change Management* 5 (2005): 378.

3   Malcolm Higgs and Deborah Rowland, "All Changes Great and Small: Exploring Approaches to Change and Its Leadership," *Journal of Change Management* 5, no. 2 (2005): 121–51; and John P. Kotter, *A Force for Change: How Leadership Differs from Management* (New York: Free Press, 1990).

4   Higgs and Rowland, "All Changes Great and Small."

5   Peter M. Senge, *The Fifth Discipline: The Art and Practice of the Learning Organization* (London: Century Business, 1991); and Jeffrey K. Liker and James K. Franz, *The Toyota Way to Continuous Improvement : Linking Strategy and Operational Excellence to Achieve Superior Performance* (New York: McGraw-Hill, 2011).

6   John P. Kotter, *Leading Change* (Boston: Harvard Business School Press, 1996); and Michael Hammer and James Champy, *Reengineering the Corporation: A Manifesto for Business Revolution* (New York: HarperBusiness, 1993).

7   Leandro Herrero, "Change management: Harvard, you have a problem," accessed May 21, 2015, http://leandroherrero.com/change-management-harvard-you-have-a-problem/.

8   Herrero, "Change management: Harvard, you have a problem."

MODULE 12
WHERE NEXT?

KEY POINTS

- *Leading Change* will continue to be an important book in change literature, but its importance will lessen as new methods add to our understanding of organizational change.*

- Scholars such as Julie Battilana* of Harvard Business School and others will move Kotter's ideas forward by expanding the range of study techniques and focusing on employees rather than executives.

- *Leading Change* was written at a time when change was an emerging topic and its clarity, comprehensiveness, and use of practical examples has made it a seminal work.

Potential

John P. Kotter's *Leading Change* remains a milestone in the field of organizational change. Understanding and carrying out change is seen as much more important today than it was in 1996. Businesses face new challenges every day and have to keep in touch with the latest market trends and technologies. This forces them to transform their methods, culture, and processes to keep up with global forces and competition. As long as adaptation remains a crucial aspect of business life, the principles in *Leading Change* will continue to be relevant.

The future potential of *Leading Change* is tied to the development of change models that reflect the flexible organizations of the future. Kotter predicted the emergence of flexible businesses, but business structures have transformed even more rapidly than even he imagined. One criticism of *Leading Change* has been that the model centers on the senior ranks of management* in an organization. As Kayleigh

❝Formal authority is, of course, an important source of influence. Previous research has shown how difficult it is for people at the bottom of a typical organization chart—complete with multiple functional groups, hierarchical levels, and prescribed reporting lines—to drive change. But most scholars and practitioners now also recognize the importance of the informal influence that can come from organizational networks.**❞**

Julie Battilana and Tiziana Casciaro, "The Network Effects of Great Change Agents"

O'Keefe writes: "The 8-step model puts enormous pressure on leaders and managers, but doesn't ask for much of employees. Managers are expected to ease fears, have all the answers, be expert communicators, and manage talent. Employees are expected to follow along."[1] Kotter's eight-stage model could be improved by integrating feedback from employees closer to the implementation of changes. A greater focus on uncertainty, and on employee participation in change efforts could also improve Kotter's model.

Future Directions

One scholar who may move the study of change leadership* in this direction is Julie Battilana, associate professor at Harvard Business School. Battilana's work has used network analysis—the use of graph theory and network models to study social behavior—to understand how great change leaders operate in a business. In "The Network Secrets of Great Change Agents," Battilana and her co-author Tiziana Casciaro used a social network model to study 68 change initiatives in the National Health Service* in the United Kingdom. The model looks at individuals in the organization and how they are connected, allowing the authors to determine whether or not an individual is enabling change, resisting it, or is indifferent.

Their network analysis uncovered three aspects of change leadership Kotter's model does not include. First, "Change agents who were central in the organization's informal network had a clear advantage, regardless of their position in the formal hierarchy."[2] In other words, individuals who are well connected in a company can be crucial for change even if they do not have formal power. Second, individuals who "bridged disconnected groups," (groups that otherwise would not be connected) were better at implementing major changes, while individuals with "cohesive networks" (networks in which most or all of the individuals are connected) were better at bringing about minor changes. Finally, maintaining associations with "fence-sitters," or individuals "ambivalent about a change," was beneficial for carrying out change efforts. In contrast, maintaining associations with resistors could reduce the probability that a change effort will be successful. This research begins to fulfill the potential aim of *Leading Change*—to understand at the level of the individual how change efforts flow through an organization. Network analysis can replace Kotter's discussion of leading coalitions with a more rigorous investigation of how coalitions work and what kinds of personalities form them.

Summary

Since its publication, *Leading Change* has had considerable influence in both the classroom and the boardroom. It is one of the dominant perspectives on how organizations think about change efforts in large organizations. The combination of Kotter's practical eight-step model and his numerous examples make the book a useful guide for potential leaders at any level. For two decades, the book has had a powerful influence on how managers think about organizational transformation; knowledge of *Leading Change* should enable students to interact more effectively with their managers on entering the workforce.

Leading Change was written at a time when organizations were just beginning to recognize the importance of change in their organizations. Since then, change has become an ever-present feature of the business environment. Kotter presents his work in a very simple, approachable, and comprehensible way. The book identifies common mistakes that managers make that hinder change: when managers read the book, they can relate to the mistakes and find similarities with their own experience. This conversational tone is *Leading Change's* defining feature and ensures that readers at all levels will find the book not only useful, but also enjoyable.

NOTES

1   Kayleigh O'Keefe, "Where Kotter's 8 Steps Gets it Wrong," *CEB Blogs*, accessed May 21, 2015, https://www.executiveboard.com/blogs/where-kotters-8-steps-gets-it-wrong/.

2   Julie Battilana and Tiziana Casciaro, "The Network Secrets of Great Change Agents," *Harvard Business Review*, accessed May 21, 2015, https://hbr.org/2013/07/the-network-secrets-of-great-change-agents/ar/1.

GLOSSARY

GLOSSARY OF TERMS

Affordable Care Act (known as Obamacare): a United States statute passed in 2010 that represents the most significant reform of the American health care system since 1965. The act requires Americans to hold some kind of health insurance and established insurance exchanges to create competition in the insurance market.

Broad-based empowerment: representation and participation in decision-making among a large group of employees.

Collapse of communism: the revolutions of 1989, which resulted in the communist governments of various central and eastern European countries being overthrown. More countries became linked to the capitalist system, which led to an increase in privatization (and therefore more private corporations).

Compounded growth: a concept describing growth that is exponential or logarithmic, i.e. growth that builds on itself. The principle of compounded growth implies both personal and professional development.

Contingency factors: aspects of the business environment that influence planning and strategy, including changes in the external environment and technology.

Corporate culture: the shared values, beliefs, and behaviors of a company's employees and management. A company's corporate culture will determine how people interact within the company and how it handles its business transactions and external relationships.

Cyclical change: an approach to change leadership that emphasizes that change cannot be understood on a step-by-step basis, and offers leaders alternative guidelines for leading change.

Domestic market: the market for goods and services in a given country.

Economics: social science that studies the production, distribution, and consumption of both goods and services.

Free trade: a policy of not restricting trade between countries, usually by removing tariffs and other trade barriers.

Global 5000 companies: a database of 5000 companies, both private and public, representing several industries and more than $50 trillion in revenue.

Globalization: the process by which the world seems to become increasingly smaller. This is often the result of advances in communication and growing interactions of culture, commerce, religion, and politics among groups that normally would not have been in contact with one another.

Guiding coalition: a group of people with the ability and drive to lead a change effort in an organization.

International economic integration: this can refer to agreements such as GATT (General Agreement on Tariffs and Trade). GATT was a multilateral agreement between nations to regulate international trade. The purpose was to reduce tariffs and other trade barriers for mutual benefits among countries. GATT was signed in 1947 and lasted until 1994, when it was replaced by the World Trade Organization (WTO).

Leadership: this typically refers to a quality or set of qualities, including vision, charisma, persistence, power, and intelligence, that translate into the carrying out of effective social change. Leadership can also be the process of carrying out change by enlisting the support of others.

Leadership studies: a multidisciplinary academic discipline with the goal of identifying the characteristics of successful leadership and understanding the context of leadership in organizations.

Learning organization: a term coined by Peter Senge and his colleagues at the MIT Sloan School of Management and used in his book *The Fifth Discipline: The Art and Practice of the Learning Organization*. *The Fifth Discipline* talks about an organization that has five features: systems thinking, personal mastery, mental models, shared vision, and team learning. Learning organizations value teamwork and collaborative models of management.

Lifelong learning: the process of continually growing both personally and professionally.

Macroeconomics: the branch of economics that deals with large-scale economic factors, such as economic growth, the money supply, and long-term trends in technology.

Management: the function in businesses and organizations that coordinates the efforts of different branches of the company. Managers are typically tasked with achieving objectives in such a way that minimizes costs or effort.

Management by Objectives (MBO): an approach to management developed by Peter Drucker in which results are tied to objectives in the firm, which are, in turn, tied to managerial behavior.

Management consulting: the process of helping firms with their performance, typically by analyzing processes and strategy in the company.

Management studies: an academic discipline dedicated to understanding the internal processes of business organizations and how those processes can be changed to maximize business objectives.

MBA: short for Master of Business Administration, this is a master's degree, originally awarded in the United States in the late nineteenth century as a measure of academic excellence when industrialization started to happen.

McKinsey: refers to McKinsey & Company, a multinational management consulting firm, which produces analysis to help companies make good management decisions.

National Health Service (NHS): the publicly funded health care system of the United Kingdom.

North American Free Trade Agreement (NAFTA): a free trade agreement that went into effect in January 1994 between Mexico, Canada, and the United States. The goal of the agreement was to eliminate trade barriers between the three countries.

Organizational behavior: the study of individual and group activity in an organization.

Political science: social science that studies political institutions and processes.

Reengineering: using information technology to re-invent the way a company does its business—improving productivity and cutting costs.

Short-term wins: successes that are likely to be a step towards a larger goal rather than the ultimate goal.

Social network analysis: the use of network models and graphs to study social structures and the ways in which social structures operate in other institutions.

Technological change: this refers to faster and better communication (the Internet revolution), better means of transportation, and information networks that connect people globally.

Theory X and Theory Y model: a model of organizational behavior developed by Douglas McGregor in which managers operate using a theory—Theory X or Theory Y—to understand their employees. Under Theory X, employees are assumed to be inherently lazy, while under Theory Y they are self-motivated.

Total Quality Management: a management principle where every member of a company must commit to maintaining the highest standards possible in every area to improve customer satisfaction.

Trade regulation: a field of law covering the analysis and regulation of international trade. Particular concern is given to limiting anti-competitive practices such as unfair pricing or monopoly.

Transformative organizations: an organization that changes the way it operates in a significant way. Transformation can refer to the production process, the hiring process, or any major feature of the organization.

PEOPLE MENTIONED IN THE TEXT

Chris Argyris (1923–2013) was an American business scholar who studied the relationship between organizational structures and firm behavior. He is also associated with the development of action science, or the study of how human beings design their actions in the face of challenges.

Achilles A. Armenakis is an American business scholar who currently teaches at Auburn University. His primary research interest is change management.

Julie Battilana is a French business scholar who currently teaches at Harvard Business School. Her work focuses on how individuals and organizations can move away from deeply seated norms in order to change their behavior.

W. Warner Burke is an American professor of psychology and education at Teachers College at Columbia University. He maintains a workgroup studying the Burke-Litwin model of organizational change at Columbia.

Bernard Burnes (b. 1953) is a professor of organizational change at the Stirling Management School. His research covers the way in which different approaches to change promote or undermine ethical behavior in organizations.

James Champy (b. 1942) is a management consultant and authority on organizational change and business reengineering and renewal.

Clayton Christensen (b. 1952) is a professor at Harvard Business School and is regarded as one of the top experts on innovation and growth. His ideas have been widely used in organizations around the world.

William Edwards Deming (1900–93) was an American engineer and management consultant. He had a wide-ranging career, but one of his scholarly contributions is the Total Quality Management Movement, which is considered to have been born with his book *Out of Crisis*. In that book, Deming describes what managers should do to create lasting organizational change.

Peter Drucker (1909–2005) was an Austrian American management consultant and scholar who is considered the father of modern management. He helped develop the practical foundations of the modern business entity, and is known for his Management by Objectives (MBO) approach.

Nils Finstad is a Norwegian scholar of organizational change who has taught at Bodø Regional University.

James K. Franz is an American businessman who serves as vice president of global operations at Toyota Way Academy.

Timothy Galpin is an American management professor at Colorado State University. He also serves as a business consultant on topics ranging from strategic planning, restructuring, and organizational change.

Michael Hammer (1948–2008) was an American author and engineer whose Business Process Reengineering (BPR) approach to management has been highly influential.

Heather Haveman is an American professor of organizational theory at the University of California, Berkeley. Her work investigates how organizations, and the people in them, evolve in the face of external and internal changes.

Leandro Herrero is a consultant, clinical psychologist, and lecturer who serves as CEO of the Chalfont Project, which oversees the Viral Change initiative, dedicated to the creation and implementation of large-scale behavioral and cultural change.

Malcolm Higgs is professor of human resource management and organization behavior at Southampton Business School. His academic interests include change management, particularly the link between positive emotions and change leadership.

Arnold S. Judson is a writer and management consultant who has written on change efforts and served as president of the Judson Company Inc., a strategic management consultancy based in Boston.

Daniel Kahneman (b. 1934) is an Israeli American psychologist, professor emeritus at Woodrow Wilson School at Princeton University, and Nobel Memorial Prize Winner in Economic Sciences.

Gregg LeStage (b. 1965) is Executive Vice President of Kotter International where he is responsible for global business development as well as working directly with clients.

Kurt M. Lewin (1890–1947) was a German American psychologist, known for his pioneering work in the field of social and organizational psychology. He also provided a framework for looking at the factors (forces) that influence social situations, called Force Field Analysis. Force Field Analysis has been used in studies on organizational change to identify the relevant forces that affect the process of change.

Jeffrey K. Liker is an American professor of industrial and operations engineering at the University of Michigan, and owner of Liker Lean Advisors, a consulting firm. His work has studied the success of management techniques such as those used at Toyota.

George Litwin is an American organizational psychologist who has taught at Harvard Business School and whose work studies the characteristics of successful leaders.

Richard Luecke (b. 1943) is the author of a number of books on business and management including *Entrepreneur's Toolkit* (2004) and *The Busy Manager's Guide to Delegation* (2009).

Douglas McGregor (1906–64) was a management scholar who spent much of his career at the Massachusetts Institute of Technology. Perhaps McGregor's most important contribution was to introduce human behavior into the analysis of organizations.

Henry Mintzberg (b. 1939) is a Canadian scholar and consultant who has written several books, including *Managers not MBAs* and *Simply Managing*. His work focuses on managerial work, strategy formation, and forms of organizing.

Peter Northouse is a professor emeritus of communication in the School of Communication at Western Michigan University. His work focuses on models of leadership, leadership assessment, and group dynamics.

Barack Obama (b. 1961) is the 44th president of the United States. He is notable for being the first African American president and for introducing the first major health insurance reform act in decades, the Patient Protection and Affordable Care Act of 2010.

Macat Analysis of **John P. Kotter's** *Leading Change*

Michael Porter (b. 1947) is a professor at Harvard Business School, known for his five forces model.

Deborah Rowland is founder of Lead Free Consultancy, a firm that provides change management advice to corporations. She is also the co-author of *Sustaining Change: Leadership That Works*, a guidebook for implementing change.

Leonard Schlesinger is a professor at Harvard Business School whose work studies the role of effective leaders in organizations.

Peter Senge (b. 1947) is an American systems scientist who currently teaches at the Massachusetts Institute of Technology. He is best known for his book *The Fifth Discipline*, which developed the theory of the learning organization.

Thomas Vollmann (1937–2009) was an American business professor who was considered a leading figure in the area of manufacturing control systems.

Gary Yukl (b. 1940) is an American management scholar who teaches at the University of Albany School of Business. His academic interests include leadership, power and influence, motivation, training, and development.

WORKS CITED

WORKS CITED

Argyris, Chris. *Interpersonal Competence and Organizational Effectiveness.* Homewood, IL: Dorsey Press, 1962.

Organization and Innovation. Homewood, IL: R. D. Irwin, 1965.

Armenakis, Achilles A., and Arthur G. Bedeian. "Organizational Change: A Review of Theory and Research in the 1990s." *Journal of Management* 25 (1999): 293–315.

Armenakis, Achilles A., Stanley G. Harris, and Hubert S. Feild. "Paradigms in Organizational Change: Change Agent and Change Target Perspectives." *Public Administration and Public Policy* 87 (2001): 631–58.

Barnett, William P., and Glenn R. Carroll. "Modeling Internal Organizational Change." *Annual Review of Sociology* 21 (1995): 217–36.

Burke, W. Warner, and George H. Litwin. "A Causal Model of Organizational Performance and Change." *Journal of Management* 18, no. 3 (1992): 523–45.

Burnes, Bernard. "No Such Thing as … a 'One Best Way' to Manage Organizational Change." *Management Decision* 34, no. 10 (1996): 11–18.

By, Rune Todnem. "Organisational Change Management: A Critical Review." *Journal of Change Management* 5 (2005): 369–80.

Conner, Daryl. *Leading at the Edge of Chaos: How to Create the Nimble Organization.* New York: John Wiley, 1998.

Deming, William Edwards. *Out of the Crisis.* Cambridge, MA: MIT Press, 2000.

Finstad, Nils. "The Rhetoric of Organizational Change." *Human Relations* 51, no. 6 (1998): 717–40.

Galpin, Timothy J. *The Human Side of Change: A Practical Guide to Organization Redesign.* San Francisco: Jossey-Bass Publishers, 1996.

Hammer, Michael, and James Champy. *Reengineering the Corporation: A Manifesto for Business Revolution.* New York: HarperBusiness, 1993.

Haveman, Heather A. "Between a Rock and a Hard Place: Organizational Change and Performance Under Conditions of Fundamental Environmental Transformation." *Administrative Science Quarterly* 37, no. 1 (1992): 48–75.

Higgs, Malcolm, and Deborah Rowland. "All Changes Great and Small: Exploring Approaches to Change and Its Leadership." *Journal of Change Management* 5, no. 2 (2005): 121–51.

Judson, Arnold S. *Changing Behavior in Organizations: Minimizing Resistance to*

Change. Cambridge, MA: Blackwell, 1991.

Kotter, John P. *A Force for Change: How Leadership Differs from Management*. New York: Free Press, 1990.

"Leading Change: Why Transformation Efforts Fail." *Harvard Business Review* 73, no. 2 (1995): 59–67. Reprinted in *HBR's 10 Must Reads: On Change Management* (Boston: Harvard Business School Press, 2011).

Leading Change. Boston: Harvard Business School Press, 1996.

"Leading Change: A Conversation with John P. Kotter." *Strategy & Leadership* 25 (1997): 18–23.

The New Rules: Eight Business Breakthroughs to Career Success in the 21st century. New York: Free Press, 1997.

"Accelerate!" *Harvard Business Review* 90, 11 (2012): 43–58.

Kotter, John P., and James L. Heskett. *Corporate Culture and Performance*. New York: Free Press, 1992.

Kotter, John P., and Holger Rathgeber. *Our Iceberg Is Melting: Changing and Succeeding Under Any Conditions*. New York: St Martin's Press, 2006.

LeStage, Gregg, "How Have Kotter's Eight Steps for Change Changed." *Forbes*, March 5, 2015. Accessed June 17, 2015. http://www.forbes.com/sites/johnkotter/2015/03/05/how-have-kotters-eight-steps-for-change-changed/.

Lewin, Kurt. "Frontiers in Group Dynamics II: Channels of Group Life; Social Planning and Action Research." *Human Relations* 1 (1947): 143–53.

Liker, Jeffrey K., and James K. Franz. *The Toyota Way to Continuous Improvement : Linking Strategy and Operational Excellence to Achieve Superior Performance*. New York: McGraw-Hill, 2011.

Luecke, Richard. *Managing Change and Transition*. Boston: Harvard Business School Press, 2003.

Lunenburg, Fred C. "Leadership Versus Management: A Key Distinction—At Least in Theory." *International Journal of Management, Business and Administration* 14, no. 1 (2011): 1–4.

McGregor, Douglas, and Joel Cutcher-Gershenfeld. *The Human Side of Enterprise*. New York: McGraw-Hill, 2006.

Mintzberg, Henry. "Rebuilding Companies as Communities." *Harvard Business Review* 87, nos. 7/8 (2009): 140–3.

Moran, John W., and Baird K. Brightman. "Leading Organizational Change." *Career Development International* 6, no. 2 (2001): 111.

Northouse, Peter Guy. *Leadership: Theory and Practice*. Thousand Oaks, CA:

Sage Publications, 2004.

Pettigrew, A. M., R. W. Woodman, and K. S. Cameron. "Studying Organizational Change and Development: Challenges for Future Research." *Academy of Management Journal* 44, no. 4 (2001): 697–713.

Porter, Michael. "How Competitive Forces Shape Strategy." *Harvard Business Review* 57, no. 2 (1979): 137–45.

Senge, Peter M. *The Fifth Discipline: The Art and Practice of the Learning Organization*. London: Century Business, 1991.

The Dance of Change: The Challenges of Sustaining Momentum in Learning Organizations. New York: Currency/Doubleday, 1999.

Vollmann, Thomas E. *The Transformation Imperative: Achieving Market Dominance Through Radical Change*. Boston: Harvard Business School Press, 1996.

Yukl, Gary A. *Leadership in Organizations*. Upper Saddle River, NJ: Prentice Hall, 2010.

Zaleznik, Abraham. "Managers and Leaders: Are They Different?" *Harvard Business Review* 55, no. 5 (1977): 67–78.

THE MACAT LIBRARY
BY DISCIPLINE

The Macat Library By Discipline

AFRICANA STUDIES

Chinua Achebe's *An Image of Africa: Racism in Conrad's Heart of Darkness*
W. E. B. Du Bois's *The Souls of Black Folk*
Zora Neale Huston's *Characteristics of Negro Expression*
Martin Luther King Jr's *Why We Can't Wait*
Toni Morrison's *Playing in the Dark: Whiteness in the American Literary Imagination*

ANTHROPOLOGY

Arjun Appadurai's *Modernity at Large: Cultural Dimensions of Globalisation*
Philippe Ariès's *Centuries of Childhood*
Franz Boas's *Race, Language and Culture*
Kim Chan & Renée Mauborgne's *Blue Ocean Strategy*
Jared Diamond's *Guns, Germs & Steel: the Fate of Human Societies*
Jared Diamond's *Collapse: How Societies Choose to Fail or Survive*
E. E. Evans-Pritchard's *Witchcraft, Oracles and Magic Among the Azande*
James Ferguson's *The Anti-Politics Machine*
Clifford Geertz's *The Interpretation of Cultures*
David Graeber's *Debt: the First 5000 Years*
Karen Ho's *Liquidated: An Ethnography of Wall Street*
Geert Hofstede's *Culture's Consequences: Comparing Values, Behaviors, Institutes and Organizations across Nations*
Claude Lévi-Strauss's *Structural Anthropology*
Jay Macleod's *Ain't No Makin' It: Aspirations and Attainment in a Low-Income Neighborhood*
Saba Mahmood's *The Politics of Piety: The Islamic Revival and the Feminist Subje*ct
Marcel Mauss's *The Gift*

BUSINESS

Jean Lave & Etienne Wenger's *Situated Learning*
Theodore Levitt's *Marketing Myopia*
Burton G. Malkiel's *A Random Walk Down Wall Street*
Douglas McGregor's *The Human Side of Enterprise*
Michael Porter's *Competitive Strategy: Creating and Sustaining Superior Performance*
John Kotter's *Leading Change*
C. K. Prahalad & Gary Hamel's *The Core Competence of the Corporation*

CRIMINOLOGY

Michelle Alexander's *The New Jim Crow: Mass Incarceration in the Age of Colorblindness*
Michael R. Gottfredson & Travis Hirschi's *A General Theory of Crime*
Richard Herrnstein & Charles A. Murray's *The Bell Curve: Intelligence and Class Structure in American Life*
Elizabeth Loftus's *Eyewitness Testimony*
Jay Macleod's *Ain't No Makin' It: Aspirations and Attainment in a Low-Income Neighborhood*
Philip Zimbardo's *The Lucifer Effect*

ECONOMICS

Janet Abu-Lughod's *Before European Hegemony*
Ha-Joon Chang's *Kicking Away the Ladder*
David Brion Davis's *The Problem of Slavery in the Age of Revolution*
Milton Friedman's *The Role of Monetary Policy*
Milton Friedman's *Capitalism and Freedom*
David Graeber's *Debt: the First 5000 Years*
Friedrich Hayek's *The Road to Serfdom*
Karen Ho's *Liquidated: An Ethnography of Wall Street*

John Maynard Keynes's *The General Theory of Employment, Interest and Money*
Charles P. Kindleberger's *Manias, Panics and Crashes*
Robert Lucas's *Why Doesn't Capital Flow from Rich to Poor Countries?*
Burton G. Malkiel's *A Random Walk Down Wall Street*
Thomas Robert Malthus's *An Essay on the Principle of Population*
Karl Marx's *Capital*
Thomas Piketty's *Capital in the Twenty-First Century*
Amartya Sen's *Development as Freedom*
Adam Smith's *The Wealth of Nations*
Nassim Nicholas Taleb's *The Black Swan: The Impact of the Highly Improbable*
Amos Tversky's & Daniel Kahneman's *Judgment under Uncertainty: Heuristics and Biases*
Mahbub Ul Haq's *Reflections on Human Development*
Max Weber's *The Protestant Ethic and the Spirit of Capitalism*

FEMINISM AND GENDER STUDIES

Judith Butler's *Gender Trouble*
Simone De Beauvoir's *The Second Sex*
Michel Foucault's *History of Sexuality*
Betty Friedan's *The Feminine Mystique*
Saba Mahmood's *The Politics of Piety: The Islamic Revival and the Feminist Subject*
Joan Wallach Scott's *Gender and the Politics of History*
Mary Wollstonecraft's *A Vindication of the Rights of Woman*
Virginia Woolf's *A Room of One's Own*

GEOGRAPHY

The Brundtland Report's *Our Common Future*
Rachel Carson's *Silent Spring*
Charles Darwin's *On the Origin of Species*
James Ferguson's *The Anti-Politics Machine*
Jane Jacobs's *The Death and Life of Great American Cities*
James Lovelock's *Gaia: A New Look at Life on Earth*
Amartya Sen's *Development as Freedom*
Mathis Wackernagel & William Rees's *Our Ecological Footprint*

HISTORY

Janet Abu-Lughod's *Before European Hegemony*
Benedict Anderson's *Imagined Communities*
Bernard Bailyn's *The Ideological Origins of the American Revolution*
Hanna Batatu's *The Old Social Classes And The Revolutionary Movements Of Iraq*
Christopher Browning's *Ordinary Men: Reserve Police Batallion 101 and the Final Solution in Poland*
Edmund Burke's *Reflections on the Revolution in France*
William Cronon's *Nature's Metropolis: Chicago And The Great West*
Alfred W. Crosby's *The Columbian Exchange*
Hamid Dabashi's *Iran: A People Interrupted*
David Brion Davis's *The Problem of Slavery in the Age of Revolution*
Nathalie Zemon Davis's *The Return of Martin Guerre*
Jared Diamond's *Guns, Germs & Steel: the Fate of Human Societies*
Frank Dikotter's *Mao's Great Famine*
John W Dower's *War Without Mercy: Race And Power In The Pacific War*
W. E. B. Du Bois's *The Souls of Black Folk*
Richard J. Evans's *In Defence of History*
Lucien Febvre's *The Problem of Unbelief in the 16th Century*
Sheila Fitzpatrick's *Everyday Stalinism*

The Macat Library By Discipline

Eric Foner's *Reconstruction: America's Unfinished Revolution, 1863-1877*
Michel Foucault's *Discipline and Punish*
Michel Foucault's *History of Sexuality*
Francis Fukuyama's *The End of History and the Last Man*
John Lewis Gaddis's *We Now Know: Rethinking Cold War History*
Ernest Gellner's *Nations and Nationalism*
Eugene Genovese's *Roll, Jordan, Roll: The World the Slaves Made*
Carlo Ginzburg's *The Night Battles*
Daniel Goldhagen's *Hitler's Willing Executioners*
Jack Goldstone's *Revolution and Rebellion in the Early Modern World*
Antonio Gramsci's *The Prison Notebooks*
Alexander Hamilton, John Jay & James Madison's *The Federalist Papers*
Christopher Hill's *The World Turned Upside Down*
Carole Hillenbrand's *The Crusades: Islamic Perspectives*
Thomas Hobbes's *Leviathan*
Eric Hobsbawm's *The Age Of Revolution*
John A. Hobson's *Imperialism: A Study*
Albert Hourani's *History of the Arab Peoples*
Samuel P. Huntington's *The Clash of Civilizations and the Remaking of World Order*
C. L. R. James's *The Black Jacobins*
Tony Judt's *Postwar: A History of Europe Since 1945*
Ernst Kantorowicz's *The King's Two Bodies: A Study in Medieval Political Theology*
Paul Kennedy's *The Rise and Fall of the Great Powers*
Ian Kershaw's *The "Hitler Myth": Image and Reality in the Third Reich*
John Maynard Keynes's *The General Theory of Employment, Interest and Money*
Charles P. Kindleberger's *Manias, Panics and Crashes*
Martin Luther King Jr's *Why We Can't Wait*
Henry Kissinger's *World Order: Reflections on the Character of Nations and the Course of History*
Thomas Kuhn's *The Structure of Scientific Revolutions*
Georges Lefebvre's *The Coming of the French Revolution*
John Locke's *Two Treatises of Government*
Niccolò Machiavelli's *The Prince*
Thomas Robert Malthus's *An Essay on the Principle of Population*
Mahmood Mamdani's *Citizen and Subject: Contemporary Africa And The Legacy Of Late Colonialism*
Karl Marx's *Capital*
Stanley Milgram's *Obedience to Authority*
John Stuart Mill's *On Liberty*
Thomas Paine's *Common Sense*
Thomas Paine's *Rights of Man*
Geoffrey Parker's *Global Crisis: War, Climate Change and Catastrophe in the Seventeenth Century*
Jonathan Riley-Smith's *The First Crusade and the Idea of Crusading*
Jean-Jacques Rousseau's *The Social Contract*
Joan Wallach Scott's *Gender and the Politics of History*
Theda Skocpol's *States and Social Revolutions*
Adam Smith's *The Wealth of Nations*
Timothy Snyder's *Bloodlands: Europe Between Hitler and Stalin*
Sun Tzu's *The Art of War*
Keith Thomas's *Religion and the Decline of Magic*
Thucydides's *The History of the Peloponnesian War*
Frederick Jackson Turner's *The Significance of the Frontier in American History*
Odd Arne Westad's *The Global Cold War: Third World Interventions And The Making Of Our Times*

LITERATURE

Chinua Achebe's *An Image of Africa: Racism in Conrad's Heart of Darkness*
Roland Barthes's *Mythologies*
Homi K. Bhabha's *The Location of Culture*
Judith Butler's *Gender Trouble*
Simone De Beauvoir's *The Second Sex*
Ferdinand De Saussure's *Course in General Linguistics*
T. S. Eliot's *The Sacred Wood: Essays on Poetry and Criticism*
Zora Neale Huston's *Characteristics of Negro Expression*
Toni Morrison's *Playing in the Dark: Whiteness in the American Literary Imagination*
Edward Said's *Orientalism*
Gayatri Chakravorty Spivak's *Can the Subaltern Speak?*
Mary Wollstonecraft's *A Vindication of the Rights of Women*
Virginia Woolf's *A Room of One's Own*

PHILOSOPHY

Elizabeth Anscombe's *Modern Moral Philosophy*
Hannah Arendt's *The Human Condition*
Aristotle's *Metaphysics*
Aristotle's *Nicomachean Ethics*
Edmund Gettier's *Is Justified True Belief Knowledge?*
Georg Wilhelm Friedrich Hegel's *Phenomenology of Spirit*
David Hume's *Dialogues Concerning Natural Religion*
David Hume's *The Enquiry for Human Understanding*
Immanuel Kant's *Religion within the Boundaries of Mere Reason*
Immanuel Kant's *Critique of Pure Reason*
Søren Kierkegaard's *The Sickness Unto Death*
Søren Kierkegaard's *Fear and Trembling*
C. S. Lewis's *The Abolition of Man*
Alasdair MacIntyre's *After Virtue*
Marcus Aurelius's *Meditations*
Friedrich Nietzsche's *On the Genealogy of Morality*
Friedrich Nietzsche's *Beyond Good and Evil*
Plato's *Republic*
Plato's *Symposium*
Jean-Jacques Rousseau's *The Social Contract*
Gilbert Ryle's *The Concept of Mind*
Baruch Spinoza's *Ethics*
Sun Tzu's *The Art of War*
Ludwig Wittgenstein's *Philosophical Investigations*

POLITICS

Benedict Anderson's *Imagined Communities*
Aristotle's *Politics*
Bernard Bailyn's *The Ideological Origins of the American Revolution*
Edmund Burke's *Reflections on the Revolution in France*
John C. Calhoun's *A Disquisition on Government*
Ha-Joon Chang's *Kicking Away the Ladder*
Hamid Dabashi's *Iran: A People Interrupted*
Hamid Dabashi's *Theology of Discontent: The Ideological Foundation of the Islamic Revolution in Iran*
Robert Dahl's *Democracy and its Critics*
Robert Dahl's *Who Governs?*
David Brion Davis's *The Problem of Slavery in the Age of Revolution*

The Macat Library By Discipline

Alexis De Tocqueville's *Democracy in America*
James Ferguson's *The Anti-Politics Machine*
Frank Dikotter's *Mao's Great Famine*
Sheila Fitzpatrick's *Everyday Stalinism*
Eric Foner's *Reconstruction: America's Unfinished Revolution, 1863-1877*
Milton Friedman's *Capitalism and Freedom*
Francis Fukuyama's *The End of History and the Last Man*
John Lewis Gaddis's *We Now Know: Rethinking Cold War History*
Ernest Gellner's *Nations and Nationalism*
David Graeber's *Debt: the First 5000 Years*
Antonio Gramsci's *The Prison Notebooks*
Alexander Hamilton, John Jay & James Madison's *The Federalist Papers*
Friedrich Hayek's *The Road to Serfdom*
Christopher Hill's *The World Turned Upside Down*
Thomas Hobbes's *Leviathan*
John A. Hobson's *Imperialism: A Study*
Samuel P. Huntington's *The Clash of Civilizations and the Remaking of World Order*
Tony Judt's *Postwar: A History of Europe Since 1945*
David C. Kang's *China Rising: Peace, Power and Order in East Asia*
Paul Kennedy's *The Rise and Fall of Great Powers*
Robert Keohane's *After Hegemony*
Martin Luther King Jr.'s *Why We Can't Wait*
Henry Kissinger's *World Order: Reflections on the Character of Nations and the Course of History*
John Locke's *Two Treatises of Government*
Niccolò Machiavelli's *The Prince*
Thomas Robert Malthus's *An Essay on the Principle of Population*
Mahmood Mamdani's *Citizen and Subject: Contemporary Africa And The Legacy Of Late Colonialism*
Karl Marx's *Capital*
John Stuart Mill's *On Liberty*
John Stuart Mill's *Utilitarianism*
Hans Morgenthau's *Politics Among Nations*
Thomas Paine's *Common Sense*
Thomas Paine's *Rights of Man*
Thomas Piketty's *Capital in the Twenty-First Century*
Robert D. Putman's *Bowling Alone*
John Rawls's *Theory of Justice*
Jean-Jacques Rousseau's *The Social Contract*
Theda Skocpol's *States and Social Revolutions*
Adam Smith's *The Wealth of Nations*
Sun Tzu's *The Art of War*
Henry David Thoreau's *Civil Disobedience*
Thucydides's *The History of the Peloponnesian War*
Kenneth Waltz's *Theory of International Politics*
Max Weber's *Politics as a Vocation*
Odd Arne Westad's *The Global Cold War: Third World Interventions And The Making Of Our Times*

POSTCOLONIAL STUDIES

Roland Barthes's *Mythologies*
Frantz Fanon's *Black Skin, White Masks*
Homi K. Bhabha's *The Location of Culture*
Gustavo Gutiérrez's *A Theology of Liberation*
Edward Said's *Orientalism*
Gayatri Chakravorty Spivak's *Can the Subaltern Speak?*

PSYCHOLOGY

Gordon Allport's *The Nature of Prejudice*
Alan Baddeley & Graham Hitch's *Aggression: A Social Learning Analysis*
Albert Bandura's *Aggression: A Social Learning Analysis*
Leon Festinger's *A Theory of Cognitive Dissonance*
Sigmund Freud's *The Interpretation of Dreams*
Betty Friedan's *The Feminine Mystique*
Michael R. Gottfredson & Travis Hirschi's *A General Theory of Crime*
Eric Hoffer's *The True Believer: Thoughts on the Nature of Mass Movements*
William James's *Principles of Psychology*
Elizabeth Loftus's *Eyewitness Testimony*
A. H. Maslow's *A Theory of Human Motivation*
Stanley Milgram's *Obedience to Authority*
Steven Pinker's *The Better Angels of Our Nature*
Oliver Sacks's *The Man Who Mistook His Wife For a Hat*
Richard Thaler & Cass Sunstein's *Nudge: Improving Decisions About Health, Wealth and Happiness*
Amos Tversky's *Judgment under Uncertainty: Heuristics and Biases*
Philip Zimbardo's *The Lucifer Effect*

SCIENCE

Rachel Carson's *Silent Spring*
William Cronon's *Nature's Metropolis: Chicago And The Great West*
Alfred W. Crosby's *The Columbian Exchange*
Charles Darwin's *On the Origin of Species*
Richard Dawkin's *The Selfish Gene*
Thomas Kuhn's *The Structure of Scientific Revolutions*
Geoffrey Parker's *Global Crisis: War, Climate Change and Catastrophe in the Seventeenth Century*
Mathis Wackernagel & William Rees's *Our Ecological Footprint*

SOCIOLOGY

Michelle Alexander's *The New Jim Crow: Mass Incarceration in the Age of Colorblindness*
Gordon Allport's *The Nature of Prejudice*
Albert Bandura's *Aggression: A Social Learning Analysis*
Hanna Batatu's *The Old Social Classes And The Revolutionary Movements Of Iraq*
Ha-Joon Chang's *Kicking Away the Ladder*
W. E. B. Du Bois's *The Souls of Black Folk*
Émile Durkheim's *On Suicide*
Frantz Fanon's *Black Skin, White Masks*
Frantz Fanon's *The Wretched of the Earth*
Eric Foner's *Reconstruction: America's Unfinished Revolution, 1863-1877*
Eugene Genovese's *Roll, Jordan, Roll: The World the Slaves Made*
Jack Goldstone's *Revolution and Rebellion in the Early Modern World*
Antonio Gramsci's *The Prison Notebooks*
Richard Herrnstein & Charles A Murray's *The Bell Curve: Intelligence and Class Structure in American Life*
Eric Hoffer's *The True Believer: Thoughts on the Nature of Mass Movements*
Jane Jacobs's *The Death and Life of Great American Cities*
Robert Lucas's *Why Doesn't Capital Flow from Rich to Poor Countries?*
Jay Macleod's *Ain't No Makin' It: Aspirations and Attainment in a Low Income Neighborhood*
Elaine May's *Homeward Bound: American Families in the Cold War Era*
Douglas McGregor's *The Human Side of Enterprise*
C. Wright Mills's *The Sociological Imagination*

Thomas Piketty's *Capital in the Twenty-First Century*
Robert D. Putman's *Bowling Alone*
David Riesman's *The Lonely Crowd: A Study of the Changing American Character*
Edward Said's *Orientalism*
Joan Wallach Scott's *Gender and the Politics of History*
Theda Skocpol's *States and Social Revolutions*
Max Weber's *The Protestant Ethic and the Spirit of Capitalism*

THEOLOGY

Augustine's *Confessions*
Benedict's *Rule of St Benedict*
Gustavo Gutiérrez's *A Theology of Liberation*
Carole Hillenbrand's *The Crusades: Islamic Perspectives*
David Hume's *Dialogues Concerning Natural Religion*
Immanuel Kant's *Religion within the Boundaries of Mere Reason*
Ernst Kantorowicz's *The King's Two Bodies: A Study in Medieval Political Theology*
Søren Kierkegaard's *The Sickness Unto Death*
C. S. Lewis's *The Abolition of Man*
Saba Mahmood's *The Politics of Piety: The Islamic Revival and the Feminist Subject*
Baruch Spinoza's *Ethics*
Keith Thomas's *Religion and the Decline of Magic*

COMING SOON

Chris Argyris's *The Individual and the Organisation*
Seyla Benhabib's *The Rights of Others*
Walter Benjamin's *The Work Of Art in the Age of Mechanical Reproduction*
John Berger's *Ways of Seeing*
Pierre Bourdieu's *Outline of a Theory of Practice*
Mary Douglas's *Purity and Danger*
Roland Dworkin's *Taking Rights Seriously*
James G. March's *Exploration and Exploitation in Organisational Learning*
Ikujiro Nonaka's *A Dynamic Theory of Organizational Knowledge Creation*
Griselda Pollock's *Vision and Difference*
Amartya Sen's *Inequality Re-Examined*
Susan Sontag's *On Photography*
Yasser Tabbaa's *The Transformation of Islamic Art*
Ludwig von Mises's *Theory of Money and Credit*

Macat Disciplines

Access the greatest ideas and thinkers across entire disciplines, including

MAN AND THE ENVIRONMENT

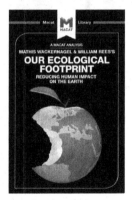

The Brundtland Report's, *Our Common Future*
Rachel Carson's, *Silent Spring*
James Lovelock's, *Gaia: A New Look at Life on Earth*
Mathis Wackernagel & William Rees's, *Our Ecological Footprint*

Macat analyses are available from all good bookshops and libraries.

Access hundreds of analyses through one, multimedia tool.
Join free for one month **library.macat.com**

Macat Disciplines

Access the greatest ideas and thinkers across entire disciplines, including

THE FUTURE OF DEMOCRACY

Robert A. Dahl's, *Democracy and Its Critics*
Robert A. Dahl's, *Who Governs?*
Alexis De Toqueville's, *Democracy in America*
Niccolò Machiavelli's, *The Prince*
John Stuart Mill's, *On Liberty*
Robert D. Putnam's, *Bowling Alone*
Jean-Jacques Rousseau's, *The Social Contract*
Henry David Thoreau's, *Civil Disobedience*

Macat analyses are available from all good bookshops and libraries.

Access hundreds of analyses through one, multimedia tool.
Join free for one month **library.macat.com**

Macat Disciplines

Access the greatest ideas and thinkers across entire disciplines, including

TOTALITARIANISM

Sheila Fitzpatrick's, *Everyday Stalinism*
Ian Kershaw's, *The "Hitler Myth"*
Timothy Snyder's, *Bloodlands*

Macat analyses are available from all good bookshops and libraries.

Access hundreds of analyses through one, multimedia tool.
Join free for one month **library.macat.com**

Macat Pairs

Analyse historical and modern issues from opposite sides of an argument. Pairs include:

RACE AND IDENTITY

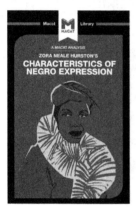

Zora Neale Hurston's
Characteristics of Negro Expression

Using material collected on anthropological expeditions to the South, Zora Neale Hurston explains how expression in African American culture in the early twentieth century departs from the art of white America. At the time, African American art was often criticized for copying white culture. For Hurston, this criticism misunderstood how art works. European tradition views art as something fixed. But Hurston describes a creative process that is alive, ever-changing, and largely improvisational. She maintains that African American art works through a process called 'mimicry'—where an imitated object or verbal pattern, for example, is reshaped and altered until it becomes something new, novel—and worthy of attention.

Frantz Fanon's
Black Skin, White Masks

Black Skin, White Masks offers a radical analysis of the psychological effects of colonization on the colonized.

Fanon witnessed the effects of colonization first hand both in his birthplace, Martinique, and again later in life when he worked as a psychiatrist in another French colony, Algeria. His text is uncompromising in form and argument. He dissects the dehumanizing effects of colonialism, arguing that it destroys the native sense of identity, forcing people to adapt to an alien set of values—including a core belief that they are inferior. This results in deep psychological trauma.

Fanon's work played a pivotal role in the civil rights movements of the 1960s.

Macat analyses are available from all good bookshops and libraries.

Access hundreds of analyses through one, multimedia tool.
Join free for one month **library.macat.com**

Macat Pairs

Analyse historical and modern issues from opposite sides of an argument. Pairs include:

INTERNATIONAL RELATIONS IN THE 21ST CENTURY

Samuel P. Huntington's
The Clash of Civilisations

In his highly influential 1996 book, Huntington offers a vision of a post-Cold War world in which conflict takes place not between competing ideologies but between cultures. The worst clash, he argues, will be between the Islamic world and the West: the West's arrogance and belief that its culture is a "gift" to the world will come into conflict with Islam's obstinacy and concern that its culture is under attack from a morally decadent "other."

Clash inspired much debate between different political schools of thought. But its greatest impact came in helping define American foreign policy in the wake of the 2001 terrorist attacks in New York and Washington.

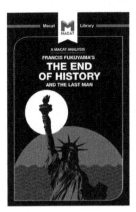

Francis Fukuyama's
The End of History and the Last Man

Published in 1992, *The End of History and the Last Man* argues that capitalist democracy is the final destination for all societies. Fukuyama believed democracy triumphed during the Cold War because it lacks the "fundamental contradictions" inherent in communism and satisfies our yearning for freedom and equality. Democracy therefore marks the endpoint in the evolution of ideology, and so the "end of history." There will still be "events," but no fundamental change in ideology.

Macat analyses are available from all good bookshops and libraries.

Access hundreds of analyses through one, multimedia tool.
Join free for one month **library.macat.com**

Printed in the United States
by Baker & Taylor Publisher Services